The Ethics of Animal Labor

Jocelyne Porcher

The Ethics of Animal Labor

A Collaborative Utopia

palgrave
macmillan

Jocelyne Porcher
Campus SupAgro
INRA, UMR 0951 Innovation Campus SupAgro
Montpellier Cedex 2, France

ISBN 978-3-319-49069-4 ISBN 978-3-319-49070-0 (eBook)
DOI 10.1007/978-3-319-49070-0

Library of Congress Control Number: 2016963263

Printed on acid-free paper

This Palgrave Macmillan imprint is published by Springer Nature
The registered company is Springer International Publishing AG
The registered company address is: Gewerbestrasse 11, 6330 Cham, Switzerland

Preface

When I began to work as a researcher into animal husbandry at the end of the 1990s, I studied animal husbandry, the profession of farming and farm animals in France, as I knew the history of animal husbandry in my country. I knew the environment, the local challenges, the different actors and the power relations. I first studied inter-subjective relations between farmers and animals, in particular the place of affectivity and suffering generated by the suppression of affective ties through the industrialisation of work. I studied the close relations humans have with each other and with animals, in a specific environment and with a specific local history, because relations between dairy farmers and their animals are not really the same in Brittany (in the west of France) as they are in Comté (in the East). The breeds of cow, the farming system and the climate are all different, the living conditions of the animals are not the same, and the marketing of milk is not the same either. This is also true of pig farming and the differences between production systems in Brittany—where more than half the pigs in France are farmed in industrial systems—and regions like the Pays Basque or the Bigorre, where local pig breeds are farmed in very close relations with nature. The differences are strongly rooted in the history of the regions, and in the ties farmers have with their animals and with their land.

However, we cannot study animal husbandry in France without considering the European and international dimension. In terms of economics, it is unarguably necessary, as the decisions that have the greatest impact on farmers are not taken in France but on a European level, and these decisions themselves depend on power relations within international markets.

It is equally necessary to extend research into relations between farmers and animals in other European countries, even in countries outside Europe (although this is more difficult), precisely because of such strong interactions between history, the environment, humans and animals.

Nevertheless, it was through researching specific subjects such as animal slaughter that I came to consider the universal character of relations between farmers and animals. Even though there are differences between farmers, be they French, Italian, Swedish, English or American, they all have in common the same moral ties in work relations with their animals. This is why research subjects such as animal slaughter can be studied and applied across borders. Relations between farmers and animals transcend the limits of nations; indeed, working with animals is a common language which is used everywhere in the world. The problems tied to the industrialization of livestock farming are the same, even if they take different forms in the USA, China or Europe. To understand the meaning of working in animal husbandry in France is to understand its meaning everywhere else too. In order to allow their animals to escape the violence of abattoirs, French, American, Swedish and Mongolian farmers are demanding that they slaughter their animals on their farms, on the basis of the same ethical ties between humans and animals at work.

The research that I reproduce the results of in this book is mainly French, but in the course of my research I also came to know the work of others in this field, including Rhoda Wilkie (2010) and Timothy Pachirat (2013) on abattoirs, Chris Bear and Lewis Holloway (2014) or Lindsay Hamilton and Nick Taylor (2013) on relations between farmers and animals and others such as Linda Kalof (2011). Research publications on relations between humans and animals are growing exponentially in social sciences at an international level, as they are in each country, where researchers also publish in their mother tongue. Such an abundance of work is both good and bad news: it is good news because it bears witness to a new interest in animals amongst social science researchers, but it is bad news because some research forgets that although as humans, "nothing human is foreign to me", as Terence wrote, this does not apply when animals are considered. We are not cows; neither are we pigs or dogs; and all cows, pigs and dogs are foreign to us. We do not live in the same world and it is one of the riches of animal husbandry that through working with animals, we are able to enter the worlds of cows, pigs and dogs. Work is the space where our worlds overlap. Cows are inserted into the human world of work and farmers enter into the world of cows, just as is the case with horses in an equestrian centre, elephants in a circus, giraffes in a zoo and guide dogs for the blind. Work creates a shared world for animals and for us.

This irreducible otherness is a challenge for social sciences but it is more of a problem in applied ethology concerning farm animals. Experimentation, particularly in "animal welfare" is very often designed round the idea that pigs or cows do not participate in the process of experimentation. The researcher makes hypotheses that the actions of an animal in stages one, two or three of the experiment depend on the conditions in which the animal is placed and these actions have sense to the researcher in relation to their hypotheses. In this way, the researcher can say that a difference is statistically significant and it is proof that, for example, chickens or pigs prefer one thing or the other, without any reference to ties to the real living conditions of animals at work and above all, without consideration of animal subjectivity, of an animal's own intelligence in the situation and the inter-subjective relations which inevitably bind it to work. This is why some researchers, conscious of these limitations, have thought of alternatives to experiments in research into "animal welfare" which seek to access what animals feel. This is, for example, the objective of research leading from quantitative behavioural assessment approaches which access animal emotions through how humans view them.

By seeking to understand animal emotions, capacities and will, we can tackle the question of their ties to work seriously. We and domestic animals have not lived together for thousands of years on a whim from which we can easily disentangle ourselves without consequences; we work together. The challenge of work is a major condition of life for animals, just as it is for us. Work is the hyphen (-) which unites the human-animal partnership; it is a tiny symbol, but it carries huge questions.

Bibliography

Hamilton L., Taylor N., 2013. Animals at work: identity, politics and culture in work with animals. Human animal studies series. Brill

Holloway L., Bear C., 2014. Recapturing bovine life: robot-cows relationships, freedom and control on dairy farming. Journal of Rural Studies, Vol. 33, pp. 131–140

Kalof L., Montgomery G.M. (eds.), 2011. Making animal meaning. Michigan State University Press

Pachirat T., 2013. Every twelve seconds. Industrialized slaughter and the politics of sight. Yale agrarian studies series. Yale University Press

Phytian C.J., Michalopoulou E., Cripps P.J., Duncan J.S., Wemelfelder F., 2016. On-farm qualitative behaviour assessment in sheep: Repeated measurements across time, and association with physical indicators of flock health and welfare. Applied Animal Behaviour Science, Vol. 175, pp. 23–31

Wilkie R.M., 2010. Livestock/deadstock. Working with farm animals from birth to slaughter. Animal, culture and societies series. Temple University Press

Contents

Introduction

> Madonna had given birth at the beginning of the night. When I returned to the sheep farm, her lamb, nestling against its mother, looked at me mischievously. "Hello sweetie", I said to it, and I took its soft, warm little body in my arms. Madonna took advantage of this to get up and shake herself. I was delighted that the lamb was a female. It was the first birth of the season and the girls seemed to rejoice as I did. "Shall we go, my lovelies?" I opened the gate and they came tumbling out, moved as much to play as they were moved by the desire to run, jump and indulge in brief but ostentatious battles. Madonna's little one fed tranquilly. I asked myself what I should call her. She had a mischievous air that I liked: *Friponne*[1] maybe? The dog dragged me from my thoughts by looming up in front of me, serious and effective, already fully engaged in his work. "Hey you, where's the fire?" I exclaimed on seeing his intention, but he was already far away, and the ewes, under his authority, were in an orderly line, *La Vieille Corne*[2] in front.

What value does my own beautiful and sensual experience with animals have, an experience shared by thousands of other livestock farmers as I have shown in my research with them, at a time when animal husbandry is condemned in the name of the environment and "animal liberation"; when "the livestock industry" brutalizes animals in the name of economic rationale and profit; when, in the name of compassion or of pragmatism, we are inclining towards preferring living death to life?

[1] Translator's note: endearing, feminine term, the equivalent of "scamp", or "rascal".
[2] Translator's note: "Old Lady".

Since the nineteenth century, industrial capitalism has seized work relations with animals from animal husbandry, and has made it the concern of the livestock industry. Farmers have been caught in a never-ending race by productivism and the obsessive search for there to be "ever more": more milk, more piglets, more lambs, ever more quickly, and ever more profitably for investors in the meat, agri-food, pharmaceutical, genetic, building and banking industries. Although at the end of the war, modernizers promised better days for farming, it is now obvious that it was not the best which was coming, but the worst. Modernizers[3] promised general well-being thanks to the indefinite growth of production, but these days, the most shared product of the livestock industry is suffering. According to Serge Latouche (2011), the rise in gross domestic product in our societies has gone hand in hand with a degradation in human relations and a net decline in the feeling of being happy; in work with farm animals too, relations with animals have declined dramatically. In unison with the improvement in performance, the pleasure of being with animals has vanished into columns of figures and productivity calculations. However, animal husbandry has nothing to do with the livestock industry. Contrary to the most frequent assertions, there is no logical and irreducible line which, in the march of time and of progress, has advanced from an archaic to a modern relationship with farm animals. Animal husbandry is a work relation with animals which is 10,000 years old, and which continues to exist worldwide, sometimes against all odds, even though the livestock industry has now been with us for 150 years, and represents one of the most greedy and harmful off-shoots of industrial capitalism.

Zootechnics, or the "science of exploiting animal machines", was born of industrial capitalism. Why, thought the industrialists, leave those sources

[3] Rene Dumont, while he was Councillor for the Agricultural Planning Commission, wrote as follows: "we are creating an organization which will provide for expansion: the rapid, progressive and harmonious development of production where man manages the economy with the mentality of a consumer: viewing economic facts from this angle, he will want to increase all production, and reduce production costs. He will ardently defend the collective interest. However, he will enter into conflict with the general interest when he is given the perspective of producer: he will tend to reduce his activity in order to increase his gain: Therefore government must give the preponderant voice to consumer representatives and connectivity. It is here where the superiority of the whole organization of inter-professional, therefore restrictive, producers lies. The peasants will be able to demand an extension of industrial production which would allow them to share in modern methods of work and greater comfort. In return they will be able to provide an abundance of food which will no longer compromise their earnings in a stable price economy, on the contrary.

of immense profit that are nature and animals in the hands of peasants? In appropriating work relations with farm animals, zootechnics radically changed the objectives, content and rules of working with animals. The animals, which had been partners in peasant work, became machines in the same way as blast furnaces, and therefore productivity had to be increased in order to increase profits. The affective and aesthetic relationship peasants had with animals was stigmatised. In his treatise on zootechnics,[4] Sanson observed that zootechnics "aims for use and not beauty", because, "it concerns making profits. For zootechnics, the best animal is not the one which would be recognized as the most beautiful in a competition judging aesthetic value, but rather the one that makes the best returns, and therefore is the most profitable to exploit" (Sanson 1907). With this intent, the declared goal of zootechnics was to turn animals into imbeciles, and to make them "automatons that carry out no other orders than those that are demanded of them" (Dechambre 1928).

The utilitarian relationship with animals built on the foundations of nineteenth-century zootechnics, paradoxically in the name of modernity and progress, endures today, and it is based on contempt and denial of humans as much as of animals. For the denial of the affectivity and existence of animals and the deleterious conditions of life at work that humans and animals suffer in common is already relatively well known to have a disastrous effect on animals, but it also has a disastrous effect on farmers and on farm workers. The gulf between procedures imposed by the industrial organization of work and the moral values of workers is an area of profound ethical suffering. For many, work in animal production has become death work. The recurrent mass slaughters of animals "destroyed" for reasons of public health and economics is an obvious example. Faced with this lethal change in our relations with animals, some members of the public demand "welfare" for animals, or, more radically, "liberation". Yet the theoretical question of "animal welfare" which appeared in France in the 1980s, although it seems attractive at first, does not seek to propose other methods of farming, but rather, to make "animal welfare" compatible with productivity, that is to say, to make the livestock industry socially acceptable. This is why, after 30 years of research and consequent implementation of "animal welfare", the conditions of life at work for farm animals have not improved; rather, they have even become considerably worse. We have effectively passed from visible suffering to invisible

[4]The complete five-volume edition was published in 1888.

suffering hidden behind good intentions and technological innovations. Behind the misery-hiding legislation, the violence and cruelty of the procedures remain. Moreover, for the supporters of "animal liberation", work relations with animals have been founded on exploitation relations since the start, and cannot be anything else. We must therefore liberate animals from all human subjugation; in other words, effect a rupture between ourselves and animals that is as radical as it is definitive; this rupture must not be limited to farm animals but must include "pet" animals as well, as they too are considered as victims of our domination. This break with animals is also supported by industrialists, who, in consideration of difficulties with the slaughter and processing of animals experienced these days, would prefer to move away from farm animals towards the production of animal matter. This is why an animal protection organization such as People for the Ethical Treatment of Animals (PETA) in the USA, following from current thinking on animal ethics, supports biologists who are working on in vitro meat production.

Living with animals has become a utopia, an impossible country; it is impossible because of the profoundly unequal balance of power between the big hegemonic industrial groups worldwide and the individual and collective goodwill of millions of farm workers and ordinary people who aspire to have another relationship with animals and with nature, at work and in life, and who declare far and wide that another world is possible.

Running through all the stories gleaned from my adventures with animals and their farmers is a redefinition of our relations with domestic animals that I want to invite the reader to consider. What is animal husbandry? What are the differences between husbandry and the livestock industry? Why kill animals? What is the purpose of "animal welfare"? Should we liberate animals? How can we, in the twenty-first century, overcome the logic of the livestock industry, how can we dispense with the industrialization of the execution of animals while continuing to eat meat, while re-establishing a farming relationship that is consistent with our sensitivities and aspirations, as well as those of the animals? To all these questions, I will try to bring elements of answers and discussions, highlighted by my personal experience and by almost 15 years of research in the field of animal husbandry.

Bibliography

Dechambre P., 1928. Traité de zootechnie. Librairie agricole de la maison rustique - Librairie des sciences agricoles

Latouche S. 2011. Les voies de la décroissance. Pour une société d'abondance frugale. In Dans Caillé A., Humbert M., Latouche S., Viveret P, 2011. De la convivialité. Dialogues sur la société conviviale à venir. La Découverte

Sanson A., 1907. Traité de zootechnie. Tome I. Librairie agricole de la Maison rustique. Cinquième édition

CHAPTER 1

What Is Animal Husbandry?

I left Paris for the countryside in 1981. I was 25 years old. I was a secretary in a big business and up until then, I had never in my life left Paris for more than a few months, during the summer holidays. I knew nothing of the world of farming, nothing of agriculture and nothing of animal husbandry. I found a job as an accounting secretary in a SME making jeans that was starting up in my area, and at the same time I started to do as my warmly-welcoming elderly peasant neighbours did. Rather than buying vegetables, why not cultivate them in the garden? Rather than buying eggs, why not have hens, or, for that matter, chickens and rabbits for meat? Little by little I installed a vegetable garden, set up a poultry yard and learned to care for, kill, pluck and skin animals, thanks to my

Animal husbandry is one of a number of possible translations of the French word *élevage:* these include "the livestock industry", "livestock production", "livestock sector" and very often the term "livestock" which denotes both farm animals (*animals élevage*) and *élevage* itself in its productive relationship with animals. The terms "livestock industry" and "livestock production" suggest what I would call *"production animals"*, or intensive, industrialized farming. Another translation is "breeding", which emphasizes the reproduction of animals, but it seems to me that " animal husbandry" carries the sense that I give to "*élevage*", as it puts the relationship with animals, the notion of responsibility, the connotation of care, and its historical character to the forefront. The root "husband" suggests to me the French idea of the "*bon père de famille*" (good family man), that is, of responsible and sustainable management.

J. Porcher, *The Ethics of Animal Labor*,
DOI 10.1007/978-3-319-49070-0_1

neighbours and my farming friends. I progressively came to understand where what I had up till then eaten without question actually came from. For me to eat rabbit, chicken or goose at Christmas, it was necessary for the animals to be born, and for me to rear them and kill them—not kill *any* rabbit, but *my* rabbits, *my* chickens, *my* geese. Was this right? Was this just? For our neighbours, without question, that was just the way things were. For me, it was not so straightforward.

Discoveries and Lessons

After meeting some goat farmers whose farm was nearby, and to whom I subsequently gave a hand from time to time, the idea that I could abandon the job of a secretary for that of a farmer of animals grew on me. My job at the textile factory was only to make ends meet, and I thought about quitting it with pleasure, for my real life started when I left the factory for the day. I had started to work with the goats at every available opportunity. I had learned how to deliver them, to milk them and to tend them. I had learned to work with animals and I was in my element. I bought some Corsican milk-producing ewes that I had fallen for at first sight, installed a sheep pen and found some land to rent. The flock grew progressively, and the house became a little farm.

I worked as a livestock farmer for some years. My training was short[1] and done on the job, but I found animal husbandry came naturally to me. I had a "feeling" for it, as the residents of the hamlet told me; but I asked myself why I had this feeling. What created it? I liked the work enormously, and while practising it, I thought about the nature of the work, its moral challenges and what guided my choices. So instead of selling suckling lambs when they were first weaned at one month, as is usually done in the Corsican dairy system, because I felt incapable of killing them myself or having them killed I preferred to wean them sooner, feed them with artificial milk, and keep them longer, which allowed me to face up to their death and which produced excellent meat. Like all the farmers that I knew, I worried a lot about the welfare of my animals; I was responsible for them. I had an enormous amount of work, and like many farmers, I would not have made ends meet if I had been alone, but I got great

[1] I only passed a *BPA (Brevet Professionnel Agricole*—diploma in professional farming) in order to contribute to the *MSA (Mutualiste Sociale Agricole*, or national insurance for farmers).

pleasure from doing the work. Existence for me had taken on another dimension. It had changed in intensity.

Following the break-up of a relationship, not unrelated to the constraints of my work, I had to quit it all. I was asking myself what path I should follow when I learned that as a farmer I was entitled to vocational training for a change of career. As a consequence I went to Brittany with CFPPA[2] to do a BTA.[3]

At 34 years of age, I returned to school to study French, history, mathematics and biology. This is not the place to go into how interesting continuing education is for people who, by choice or by necessity, have had to change their careers, but I must pay tribute in passing to the dedication of the teaching professionals that I met throughout my return to study. At the end of this BTA, we had to complete a training course and write a short thesis. By accident or by necessity, I found myself in an industrial pig farm. It was a shock, and it continued to shock me later, when I worked, this time by necessity, on two pig farms during a break between two training courses. After having rubbed shoulders with goats and ewes who were individualized and respected, I found myself confronted with sows caged in buildings where there was no difference between day and night, where breathing without suffering was impossible, where there were "farmers" who had no thought for anything except money, who beat the animals to get them from one area to another, who called them "*enculés*" and "*connards*",[4] and who seemed to aspire to nothing more in life than a new car, and to be considered the elite amongst farmers. They were not unique, it is true, and during this year I came to understand that industrial farmers were managed, and what the objectives of this management were. There was a succession of technicians on the farm, selling one thing or another on the pretext of improving ventilation or feeding. Others encouraged the farmer to upsize, to invest, their speeches almost always ending in "think about it, you're the boss", although, on the contrary, discussions showed that the "boss" was the dependant, and did not really have any choice.

In Brittany I had arrived, I thought, in a traditional animal husbandry area. They weren't amateurs like myself and the peasants and small-scale farmers of animals that I had known no doubt, they were pros by their

[2] Translator's note: *Centre de Formation Professionnelle et de Promotion Agricole* (Centre for Agricultural Professional Training in, and Promotion of, Agriculture).

[3] Translator's note: *brevet de technicien agricole* (tertiary diploma in agriculture).

[4] Translators note: vulgar expletives, the equivalent of "asshole", or "fucker".

own account; and yet to me, what they did was incomprehensible. So this was what you could call livestock farming? *Real* livestock farming? Writing a short thesis for the BTA gave me the opportunity to reflect for the first time on work relations with animals. If farming was like this, was there really no way of doing it differently? Would it not be better to work with sows without this productivist violence? I had never worked with pigs, I hadn't even really seen any before coming to Brittany, and yet working with them did not pose any difficulties for me. I had never beaten or mistreated an animal. I maintained this position in the different jobs that I held, and I learned as time passed that my patience was much more effective than the brutality of my colleagues. However, from their point of view, I was "sensitive", in the sense of sentimental, because I was a woman, while *they* were men, and they preferred a rubber pipe to negotiation. For my part, I asked myself if I was sensitive, if it was because of sentimentality or sensitivity that I refused to be violent with the animals, if the fact that I was a woman was something to consider in the situation. This was a question that I would research later, and the results of that research highlight the differences between men and women in relation to working with animals (Porcher 2008).

At the conclusion of the BTA, my teachers recommended that I continue with a BTS.[5] I decided to follow one on "the livestock industry", in order to complete my knowledge of animal husbandry, and I explained this to the director of the training course. "You would be better off doing a BTS in management", he answered, "The livestock industry, you know, has nothing to do with animal husbandry". This little phrase took me aback, but I realized afterwards its justice, and that it needed to be understood and explained.

Zootechnics: The "Science of the Exploitation of Animal Machines"

The livestock industry has nothing to do with animal husbandry. Nothing that I had experienced as a farmer was covered in courses on zootechnics or on agriculture. Of husbandry itself there was no mention throughout this year of training, and if I had not been a farmer of animals myself, I would not have learned much that was relevant to my field of work. My experience on pig farms, however, did make a little more sense. The livestock

[5] Translator's note: *Brevet de technicien supérieur* (advanced technician certificate).

industry is a technique and a business. Animals have no place; they are things to be technically and physically manipulated to optimize production, whether they are cows, chickens or pigs. Zootechnics does not seek to understand, it imposes a scientistic approach on to work relations with animals. It imposes this not only on students, but also on farmers. There is no route through zootechnics to a return to real work. Zootechnical ideology continues, as I have witnessed with technicians, and even opposes the experience of life. Institutional violence against animals is given as a norm, about which no questioning was possible. As a trainee in ongoing training, I was not subjected to concrete proofs of manliness (practical work such as castration or de-horning without anaesthesia), but that is not the case for students in initial training who, and I heard various accounts, experience training as a living nightmare, and a definitive turn-off to the work of livestock farming. Many managers in the livestock industry and agricultural trainers ask themselves why students desert the subject, and part of the answer lies in the incompatibility between the students' expectation of learning how to rear animals, and what they are actually taught: learning to produce them as if they were objects, and to accept the violence inherent in this production. As well as this, there is no history of zootechnics which could help to explain what happened in the past and at what moment work relations with animals became what they are today. Why has the ratio of 30 g of urea for dairy cows acquired greater importance than real life with animals?

The stranglehold that zootechnics has on concepts of work relations with livestock goes a long way towards explaining the lack of research on animal husbandry, for it has presented itself as the science of livestock farming since its origins in the middle of the nineteenth century. It has presumed to declare what livestock farming is, and it has treated it accordingly thereafter. This is why it is commonly understood today (and apparently, it is imposed as if it were evidence) that animal husbandry is "the livestock industry". It is animal husbandry improved by science. The livestock industry is the linear successor of husbandry in the march of time. The passage from animal husbandry to the industrial farming of animals has been explained by many historians, agronomic anthropologists and zootechnicians as a quasi-natural evolution. Progress, the modernization of our societies, demographic growth, technique and today, biotechnologies underscore this inevitable and beneficial transformation. Reason has won out over animal husbandry, over the Neolithic relations with nature and with animals, and we have got down to serious business. Before, there was domestication, proto-husbandry, followed by millennia of peasant animal husbandry, and now, husbandry has been taken in hand by science, that is, the livestock industry, and this signals the end of our archaic relations with animals.

Domestication and husbandry are often confused and presented as the same thing. According to the scientific majority, domestication is an effort to transform nature, intentionally or not, but either way, it is concerned with a transformation which attributes the same type of relations with plants as it does with animals, and which facilitates the "Neolithic revolution". Plant domestication and animal domestication are usually described as one and the same process, leading to animal husbandry. A minority point of view emphasizes the affective part played by ties between humans and animals that originated in the Neolithic period, and perhaps well before that (Serpell 1986; Lorenz 1985; Haudricourt 1962). However, the fact that the term "domestication" is used to describe both relations with plants and animals annuls the specificity of relations with animals, and the fact that an animal is not a plant. This is why husbandry has not been analysed as a work relationship with animals, anchored in a dynamic tie with social relations, and in the state of our relations with animals. The preponderant hypothesis of appropriation and exploitation has prevented a consideration of the liberating aspect of domestication. As stressed by Vinciane Despret in reference to the naturalist Edward Pett Thompson: "Emancipation, in the view of Thompson, is liberation from negative constraints. It is not about detachment, it is about better attachment" (Despret 2002, p. 94). It is interesting to compare Thompson's marvellous work, written in 1851, which is a veritable ode to animals, full of tenderness, with what was written in the same period by the pioneers of zootechnics. Where Thompson insisted on the intelligence and amity in our ties with animals and with nature, zootechnicians plunged us into disaffected and instrumental relations with animals and nature, and we are a long way from being free of this.

Two extracts from the relevant texts illustrate this duality in points of view:

> Human intercourse and the mode of treatment influence materially the extent to which domestication may be carried, and its operation on the animal mind. The cattle in the Tyrol possess more mind because they are treated with humanity and affection, and for the same reason, in the Swiss Alps, they are more lively and joyous amongst themselves, and more attached to their

herdsmen, than in those countries where little attention is paid to them. In some parts of Limosin, where the swine are carefully attended to, they are more cleanly, docile, and attached than is the ordinary nature of their race (…) It would be easy to deduce many more examples of the powers of training, and of the facilities of acquirement in animals, but the subject is almost too familiar, and proofs surround us on every side illustrative of the benefits we receive, of the services we gain, and of the pleasures we enjoy, by our associations with the animal world, of which even the most unthinking must be susceptible. (Thompson 1851, p. 399 and 412).

Domestic animals are machines, not in the figurative sense of the word, but in the most rigorous sense of mechanics and industry. They are machines of the same sort as the locomotives on our railways, the equipment in our factories where we distil, make sugar, weave and mould, where we transform matter into something. They are machines that provide a service and a product. Animals eat: they are machines that consume, that burn a certain quantity of fuel of a certain sort. They move. They are machines that move obediently following mechanical laws. They give milk, meat and strength: they are machines equipped to provide for a specific consumption. Animal machines are constructed on a certain plan: they are composed of determined elements—organs, as described by anatomy and mechanics. All their parts have a certain internal organization, conserve between themselves certain relations, and function by virtue of certain laws, to produce certain useful work. The activities of these machines makes up their real life, a life that physiology summarises as having four main functions: nutrition, reproduction, sentience and locomotion. These functions, which characterise life, are also conditions for our zootechnical exploitation, for consumption and yield that we must balance in a way that diminishes the actual costs in order to increase profits. (Sanson 1907, p. 4)

Zootechnics originated in the middle of the nineteenth century to a background of industry held up as an expression of human ingenuity, and a tool for wealth creation and social betterment. It was rooted in Enlightenment thought, particularly because it was seen as an exercise in reason, and zootechnicians had faith in science as a tool for knowledge and technical, social and human progress. The idea of progress inspired by Bacon and Saint Simon was a pillar of zootechnical thought and agricultural development (Sanson 1858). Eighteenth-century agricultural societies encountered by key figures of the time already had the aim of popularizing scientific progress in the eyes of the farming community. For, as Isabelle Stengers emphasized (2003, p. 297), "the alliance between science and progress is embedded in the origins of modern science. If the sciences and technology have become symbols of progress, it is because it was in the field of science that the secular figure of progress was developed during the seventeenth century, as an alternative route to salvation. The notion of progress by accumulation which, thanks to an organized collective effort, increases the sum of knowledge, had already been proposed by Bacon. To this, Boyles and Descartes added the conviction that an increase in knowledge eases the pain and misery of humanity". This is why the progress of zootechnical science was thought to support social progress.

Since its origins at the heart of industrial capitalism, zootechnics has been a tool of the industrialization of animal husbandry. It has been in the service of the livestock industry, now as in the past, with the objective of making industrial relations with animals profitable and socially acceptable, whether in relation to genetics or "animal welfare". As André Sanson wrote, domestic animals must be considered as machines, not because they really are, but because that is their function (Sanson 1907). This is why, before Sanson, de Charnacé stated "sophisticated races were born of needs that were determined in defined conditions, and followed the law of progress. The true name that we must give them is therefore *industrial races*, all others are no more than uncultivated products from uncultivated lands, poverty and ignorance" (Charnacé de 1868, p. 55).

This search for scientific knowledge ran contrary to the unsophisticated knowledge of the peasants. The spread of the economic model of work with animals was contrary to their affectivity and moral values. Nineteenth-century zootechnicians and twentieth-century modernizers both aimed to reduce the "ignorance" of the peasants, and this ignorance included their sentimental and aesthetic propensities. The ideological proximity of zootechnicians to modernizers one century apart is striking. Nineteenth-century zootechnicians' idea of progress was indeed very close to that of those who served the agricultural revolution in the 1950s (Dumont, Pisani, Debatisse). Both celebrated "the missionaries of agricultural progress" (Sanson 1858) who brought science and reason to the countryside.

The results of this "modernization", which in fact was an initiative of industrialization, are visible today: animal husbandry is held up to public scorn in a way that it could not have been even a few years ago. Hundreds of breeds of animal have disappeared, squeezed out of existence by specialization. Many cattle farmers, raised in the cult of maize-soya rations, are incapable of returning their cattle to the fields because they no longer know how to feed them with grass. This is true for the majority of pig farmers too, who, I can testify myself, are ignorant of the fact that pigs pasture on and digest grass.

Zootechnics presents itself as a scientific discipline and it is still taught as such in agricultural schools (Montméas and Jussiau 1994; Landais and Bonnemaire 1996). Yet there is no epistemology of Zootechnics—no manual, no course, no teachers specializing in its history. A course in zootechnics is essentially practical and contemporary in character. Even when zootechnics puts forward a systemic vision of livestock farming, it still stays in the here and now, without questioning what went before.[6]

Laying Down Arms

There has therefore been a radical rupture in relations with the world, between the peasant labour which continued in France up until the nineteenth century, and the work performed by contemporary industrial livestock farmers. In the time between animal husbandry being considered as a state (Mendras 1984), and it being considered as a profession or even as an activity or a series of activities as it is today, the capitalist and industrial society came into being; it resulted in the transformation (Marx), or invention (Meda 1995) of work—and in particular salaried work—as we know it today, with animals as well as in general.

Animal husbandry is a work relationship with animals. It is a relationship with 10,000 years of history, but it is important not to think of it as fossilized, or, conversely, as "modern". As shown above, the argument for modernity presents work relations with animals as a logical development which began with pastoral animal husbandry, and has evolved into "the livestock industry". Yet industrial relations with animals do not represent a modern form of animal husbandry; rather, they are only a branch of it, and one without a future. Imagine evolution as being like a bushy tree, somewhat in the style of S. J. Gould: the tree that represents animal husbandry is many thousands of years old, with thousands of long branches. It had been abundant, diverse and productive as a whole, but has recently been parasitized by an ugly gall which has spread disproportionately, hidden the light and turned the tree's resources to its profit, only to produce bitter fruit. This parasitism has weakened the tree and is bringing it to the brink

[6] On the subject of zootechnical theory and industrialization, read Porcher J., 2010. *"Cochons d'or. L'industrie porcine en questions" (Golden pigs, the swine industry in questions) Editions Quae, pp. 175–191.*

of collapse while the disfiguring gall is preparing to take root and separate itself from the dying tree, soon to flaunt its real nature without ties to the tree that it has destroyed.

Animal husbandry as it existed in the past does bear some relation with what it is today, for, as Gould pointed out, human beings have probably not changed for 40,000 or 50,000 years. This is why, as Marc Bloch explained , by listening to and understanding contemporary livestock farmers, we can retrospectively grasp the origins of animal husbandry, comprehend its transformations, and make new transformations possible, because "ignorance of the past does not confine itself to harming present knowledge, it jeopardises present action itself" (p. 25).

Animal husbandry here does not refer to a "traditional" model from a golden age which may never have existed. If animal husbandry is a bushy tree, this signifies that it is constantly transforming, and does not have an original ideal state. It exists, however, as husbandry—as human work relations with animals that are considered as such. It is necessary to note the following: (1) in living memory, "animal husbandry" has been understood as the livestock industry far more than as animal husbandry. When someone says to me "I remember when I was a child…", even if that person is more than 100 years old, they describe a profession already taken over by the industrial process; (2) animal husbandry, before the process of industrialization in the nineteenth century, denoted peasant labour where relations with animals were an integral part, especially as animals were indispensable to traction; (3) that animal husbandry belongs to the set of social relations, and that therefore it is a dynamic, and not a state. Across continents, husbandry evolved with the society within which it was rooted and was thus a microcosm of that society. Animals were not just work objects, as we will consider in more depth later, they participated in the social world, and this is exactly why husbandry is not only a production activity, but has its own issues which exceed the bounds of the food and environmental concerns to which it has too often been confined. The emergence of the industrial incarnation of livestock farming with industrial society, and the fact that this incarnation has been able to absorb husbandry to the point of its near disappearance, bears witness to the effect the diffusion of industrial relations in the world has had on our lives. The development of biotechnologies and nanotechnologies, and the enthusiasms and terrors that they give rise to, demonstrate that we are caught between a fascination with our human power to transform the world, and our inability to live in the world that we have created. To my mind, this sums up industrial farming. In theory, and to all appearances, it works. In reality, however, it does not work. Life cannot express itself and bloom in an industrial universe, because the product of industrial relations with life—is death.

Working with animals is living with animals. For better or worse, human societies were constructed with animals. Animals are part of ourselves, of our identity as human beings, in a way that is completely undervalued today, and this osmosis between the human and animal worlds reveals itself the most clearly in animal husbandry, because it is work that makes us aware of the affinities and symbiotic comprehension (Straus 2000/1935) that exist between ourselves and animals. Archaeologists, anthropologists and historians have described the place occupied by animals in human cultures across every society (Zeuner 1963; Haudricourt 1962; Serpell 1986; Ingold 1988; Sigaut 1988; Bodson 2001; Baratay and Mayaud 1997). Descola (2005) showed that the nature/culture distinction is far from being universal, and is even, in its most recent manifestation, mostly limited to the West. It is because we have separated nature and culture, humans and non-humans, that the industrialization of animals has become possible. The livestock industry is inconceivable in cosmologies such as those of the Achuars or the Makuna, as Descola described. For them, both humans and animals are people, and conversions are possible between species and within the same species.

Relations between humans and animals in industrialized countries, explicitly or not, are most often thought of within the limits of utilitarianism and contracts (Mepham 2006; Larrère and Larrère 1997), for both humans and animals, as research into animal "preferences" carried out in the field of "animal welfare" demonstrates. Animals are thought to be motivated by their short-term material interests alone, as Derwitt pointed out (1993, p. 20): "scientific and theoretical utilitarianism goes far beyond the field of social sciences and anthropology; it is not only men who are thought to be 'exclusively and principally practical utilitarians, (A. Caillé), but all living beings".

This is why I think it is a lot more productive to study the relationship between humans and animals using the gift theory (Porcher 2002b). In line with Mauss's initial intuition, Alain Caillé (2000) proposed that "the triptych of giving, receiving and returning constitutes the socio-anthropological universal, on which ancient and traditional societies are built". When considering the historical place of animals in the construction of all human societies, it is relevant to take into account their place at the heart of this triple obligation, that is, to think of animal husbandry in this "gift paradigm".

Working, with or without animals, is not only producing, it is equally *being*—being together, sharing, cooperating and creating ties (Dejours 1993). For most farmers, this "being together" with animals does not have a contractual base, but is grounded in affectivity (Porcher 2002b) and moral sense (Mouret 2009). As A. Caillé (2000) suggests, the political and moral monkey as described by F. de Waal (1995, 2010), who is capable of managing conflicts, reconciling with adversaries and empathizing, can lead us to think that the gift might have a natural basis, or that it is a shared composite of human and animal societies.

As S.J. Gould (1993, 1997), and before him Kropotkin (2002/1919) pointed out, the word "competition", employed by Darwin, and taken up by devotees of the "fight for life", was "figurative—a turn of phrase, rather than intending to denote a real fight between two groups of the same species for a means of existence" (p. 72).[7] On the contrary, for Kropotkin, it is mutual assistance that is primordial for maintaining life and the evolution of the species: "very happily, competition is not the rule in the animal kingdom, and nor is it for humanity" (p. 79). Mauss makes the same point: "Happily, as yet, not everything is classed exclusively in terms of buying and selling. Things still have a sentiment value as well as a venal value, if there really are things that only have a venal value. We do not have the morals of merchants alone (Mauss 1999/1923)".

Animal husbandry subscribes to both what Alain Caillé (1994) has called primary sociality (relationships with parents, friendship ties, ties based in love), and secondary sociality (work or voluntary work ties). Animal husbandry participates in primary sociality because relations between farmers and animals inevitably engage affectivity, the body and subjectivity. Many farmers have an emotional, amicable disposition towards their animals, which comes from representations of animals that are very close to those of humans as being living entities who are capable of emotions, and from the perception of a common capacity for experiencing pleasure and suffering. At the same time, animals participate in a farmer's work, and thus in the market economy. Working with animals guarantees the farmer an income, that is to say, it allows him to live. Economic relations with animals must therefore be integrated into exchanges relevant to the affective domain, or in other words, to primary sociality, which is primary in rela-

[7] Translated back into English from the French version.

tions and constitutes the bedrock of secondary sociality, for there would be no work with animals if farmers did not love them. Conversely, affective relationships must be integrated into exchanges that are relevant to secondary sociality. Love must not take up all the space if the farmer is to earn his living. There is no scission between these two types of sociality, rather, a fluctuation in the positioning of the farmer between one or the other, depending on both the content of the work, and the system of production.

Work with animals therefore oscillates between interest and disinterest, and between obligation and liberty; interest, because the farmer's aims are production and revenue, which are both indispensable to economic survival; disinterest, because the ties are more important than the products. Work with animals fluctuates between obligation and liberty, because the context of the relationship is work with its constraints and its rules, but equally, because these rules are not absolute, and farmers and animals alike know how to contravene them.

Animals and farmers are implicated in a cycle of "give-receive-return" at a man and beast level, and also at a family and herd-life level. The sense of life and death changes according to the level. Exchanges with animals are not contractualized and they are not uniform. Even though relations with animals in general rest on a common base, respect and exchanges are not the same with breeding animals such as cows, sows and ewes as they are with animals such as calves, lambs and piglets, which are sold more or less rapidly. Gift relations are situated in different temporalities, and circulate between herds and individuals, between different types of animals, and between life and death.

At the herd level, life circulates between man and beast. Farmers give life, and ultimately take it in order to feed human beings, that is, to maintain life. As farmers explain, animals give a lot: they give their presence, their trust, and their affection. They communicate with their farmers and they accept the rules of work. Farmers also give affection to their animals, they give respect and admiration, they do all they can to offer them a good life.

I have written previously (Porcher 2003), in collaboration with Jankélévitch, that only a good life for animals can make their death acceptable, provided the conditions of death conform with the values of the farmer: that they exclude suffering and that they have sense and coherence in the farmer's range of work. A "good death" may be a utopian representation of death, but the fact remains that death does exist and is a condition of life. Although this observation may seem trivial, it needs to be remembered. The death of animals is acceptable to us if those animals have been given a chance to live their life, and if that life has been as good as it can be, and in any case better than a life lived outside of animal husbandry would have been; if it has been more peaceful, more interesting and richer in sense and relationships than it would have been without us. Remember that the majority of farm animals, whether they be cattle, sheep, poultry or swine, are prey and not predators. Animal husbandry takes away the necessity of being "watchful beings", as suggested by Deleuze (2004). On the contrary, anyone who has witnessed cows or sheep in a barn would be able to testify that farm animals are characterized by great calm. This calm is one of the difficulties with reintroducing wolves or bears into the mountains, for as a consequence, shepherds are powerless to perform one of their undertakings to their animals: to protect them and free them from fear. Death is acceptable if the farmer respects the terms of the exchange; if the animal's life expectancy has not been reduced to almost nothing, and if the farmer, and more broadly, consumers and the population at large recognize, at least to some degree, that there was an animal. Death is acceptable if we have not arrived at it as if there was no animal, as if the animal didn't count. For farmers, therefore, the death of their animals has sense and leaves space for life: their economic life first and foremost, which is the condition of their survival as a farmer, but also the life of their herd, as the animal continues to exist in its descendants, in filiation.

A good life is the practical and rational condition for a life fulfilled. By this I do not mean constant happiness, you may as well put them all on Prozac, but a full life where the possibility of being happy—feeling joy—exists, and can be expressed. The gift of that good life is at the centre of the relational rationalities of working in animal husbandry. As Sébastien Mouret (2009) showed, it constitutes a gesture of gratitude. Farmers feel indebted to their animals, and the gift of a good life is the recognition of this debt, and a recognition of the value of the animal. This feeling is in opposition to the instrumental rationality of work.

The counter-gift the farmer offers in return for the animals' gift of their work and their lives is gratitude, which takes the form of a good life. Animal husbandry acts as a positive tide which passes from animals to men and creates a state of positive indebtedness in the farmers. This gift of a good life is not a rule for work taught in agricultural schools; in agricultural teaching, animals as such do not exist, and we are not indebted to them, nor do we have a duty to consider them. The only legal obligation we have is to assure their "welfare", which boils down to a limit on the restraints that the organization of work in the livestock industry imposes on them.

For the great majority of farmers of animals and their employees that I have met, including those working in the industrial livestock sector, whether the species involved be cattle, sheep, swine, goats or poultry, a good life for the animal is above all a tie to their own world, nature. For farmers, it is the way the world is ordered. Nature is not an anarchic pile-up of beings and things, where everything can be mixed together, as, for example, has been suggested by the geneticists who inserted fish genes into strawberries to stop them from freezing. Nature has a universal sense that must be understood and respected. This is why farm animals, which Catholic farmers in particular see as being in a hierarchical relationship with humans or in a transversal relationship of great proximity, have a legitimate place in the world, a world they also own. Specifically, give them a good life by giving them access to where they belong: to earth, grass, the sun and the rain, birdsong, wind and snow. It is by giving them the world of experiences that the individual is made to exist. This relationship we have with animals is natural and can be interpreted in different ways. We can call it "nature" or these days it can be more conveniently regrouped under "biodiversity", that is, everything that lives together, interacts, communicates, co-transforms itself and is interdependent. On the other hand, "nature" can be seen as a collective construction of humans and non-humans (Latour 1999). For the majority of farmers of animals, nature exists outside of human intentions and it manifests itself organically in the body (both their own and those of their animals), through joy and suffering, through feelings, through life and death. Nature, for many farmers of animals, is eminently sensory and sensual. It is not thought, it is felt. It is not good or bad, it exists because we do. However, although they have similar roots, humans and animals do not belong to the same category. Although humans are animals, animals are not humans, even if they are more than "non-humans", and it is this difference in proximity that allows animals to be slaughtered. The relationship between humans and animals in farming is an asymmetric relationship; workers and animals are not able to change their positions.

To work with animals is to engage in relationship of care. Farmers deliver animals and rear them. They feed them, protect them and treat them when they are sick. For many farmers, this care relationship is one of the joys of the job, but it is also a duty from a professional point of view. Whether there is a difficult birth, an animal which has fallen into a ravine or one that has been taken ill, the farmer must be present and do everything he can to help the animal. A failure in the care relationship is seen as a personal defeat and it is difficult to live with. Work relations do not exclude respect, despite the mortal fate of farm animals, because they signify, not the denial of death, but the recollection that death and life are inseparable. Before death, it is life that matters to farmers of animals.

Access to the natural world goes hand in hand with liberty of movement, social ties, nutritional diversity, the possibility of expressing the behaviour of your species (rummaging about in the dirt for a pig, grazing) and the possibility of expressing your living being (running, fighting, playing, contemplating). Thus, the gift of a good life begins with the gift of an environment where animals can live their own natural lives. Relations with nature via the fields, woods or paths are very important for cows, as well as for sows and poultry. It has a health function for the animals (walking, running, being in a herd), as well as a nutritional function. Cows get an essential part of their diet from grazing on grass and, in a natural or complex meadow, they can exercise a selective choice of plant and "eat what they like" (Meuret 2010). Equally for sows, relations to a meadow or the undergrowth are very important. Sows graze and give economic value to grass from a nutritional point of view, as well as root crops and wild plants. These relations with the meadow are also important for poultry, which can run and peck as they like. Relations between animals are an essential component of the system; cows, sows and ewes are all social animals, and it is therefore important to let them interact. These interactive relations link to those between the farmer and his animals; the farmer has working relations with the herd and relations with the individual cows just as a teacher has relations with the class and with each individual pupil. This teaching analogy is very often made by farmers, who also describe their work with animals as like an education. Remember that a young animal (a heifer) is called an *"élève"*.[8]

One difficulty with this representation, which also applies to the idea that animals have innate competences in the wild, is that it disavows a farmer's duties in the name of animal freedom. However, a good life implies protection by the farmer as well as an autonomous relationship with the natural world, which allows the animal to live in nature without being trapped by constraints such as predators, protection from the weather and

[8] Translator's note: school pupil.

the quest for food. The good life for a farm animal is not the life of a "wild" animal, and the difference is the tie with humans and the fact that the good life is part of a gift relation. The good life is the recognition of animals, it is not detachment.

The good life, therefore, is also because animals are implicated in relations with humans in the world of work, and these relations are enriching because it is animals who demand the ties. Speech and petting are the first vectors of this tie, and the majority of farmers talk to their animals. This speech is not wasted breath, it is an address; it is an address to the herd in the morning: "Hello my girls!", or at the moment of departure: "Come on, let's go!", or on returning "So, have you eaten enough?", or in the evening "See you tomorrow, grandpas.", and to each animal throughout the day: "Come here, my beauty.", "Leave it be.", or "Stop your mischief!". Further, contrary to what is often said on animal silence or lack of speech, farmers have the feeling that the animal world is very expressive, for farmers may talk, but animals say things all the time. They express themselves in their own way, baaing, bellowing and grunting, and through body language, and in a way adapted to the situation. They talk amongst themselves, and they talk to us. Pigs have many ways of grunting which do not mean at all the same thing in any given context. Animals talk amongst themselves and they talk to their farmers.

Speech between farmers and farm animals is in fact very close to speech between humans and pets, for animals look at us and listen to us, and for many farmers they understand us, and often better than we understand them. We direct human speech at animals, which is affective even without being understood to the letter; it is true we know nothing about a farm animal's ability to understand the sense of the words, although recent studies in ethology demonstrate the capacity animals, and in particular dogs, have for understand human vocabulary (Pilley and Reid 2011). It is, however, the voice producing the speech and that gives sense to the relationship (Pereira 2009).

Animals are attracted to communication with humans to a great extent because they are curious. A sense of this curiosity motivates farmers, for example, to open buildings on the side where "something is happening", where, particularly in winter when they are inside, they can see cars, people, children and other animals. Very often, incidentally, animals go where humans are, and farmers have many anecdotes about how animals show their desire to get into the house. This seems to me to speak volumes about the process of domestication. Farm animals are stakeholders in the human world, and that is why, for example, some farmers give double rations of fodder at Christmas. As Daniel Giraudon (2006) described, in Brittany, "tradition has imposed the participation of bullocks, cows and horses in particular, in the celebration of Christmas. That night they gave them fresh bedding in the stable and they had the right to an extra meal, a '*Reveillon*'[9] or '*akdoan, fiskoan*'[10] of some sort. In principal, this double ration was usually given to them before midnight mass, or on returning afterwards". Similarly, a farmer I met who hung Christmas tree balls in his barn explained, "Christmas is a time of peace anyway, for everyone. Children expect their presents, and the animals know that in winter they have to go indoors, and those who are outside are very impatient to come inside, where they find shelter as close as possible to the dry fodder."

Contrary, then, to all that can be written on "animal welfare", for farmers, the first and indispensable condition of "welfare", the one which conditions all the others, is a double relationship: a relationship with the world with access to the meadow, path and undergrowth, access to their own species and to other animals, and a relationship with humans. Quality in the animal husbandry system comes from allowing these relations.

Work has different rationalities for individuals as well as for collectives, and these are: economic (productive), identity (reproductive), relational (being together) and axiological (acting in conformity with values). These rationalities work together or conflict with each other (Porcher 2002a: Fiorelli et al 2007; Fiorelli 2010). All the results of my surveys have shown that animal husbandry, as a traditional work relationship with animals, has a relational rationality first and foremost. The majority of farmers who have chosen their profession, rather than those who just endure it, work with animals in order to live with them. Transformations in relations with some animals, such as donkeys in France and elephants in Asia, demonstrate this. The traditional work of these animals of carrying loads is no longer necessary and they have been replaced by machines. In order to continue to live with donkeys or with elephants, those who work in animal husbandry must find them other tasks, or even another job, such as taking tourists for rides.

The fact that the first rationality of working in animal husbandry is the relationship and that affectivity is invested in the work does not mean that this relationship is a bed of roses, for the work imposes strong constraints,

[9] Translator's note: the traditional Christmas Eve dinner.

[10] Translator's note: as above, in the Breton language.

and the relationship between individuals is not equal. The affectivity relationship can be described as using the two dimensions of friendship and power. Very often, work relationships with animals oscillate between two positions. One position will take precedence over the other depending on the personality of the farmer, and above all, the farming system. The results of my research show that women and farmers in non-industrial systems are more likely to be driven by affection towards their animals, and better educated farmers and those working in intensive and industrial systems are more driven by power. Interestingly, the results show that older people are positive in the dimensions of affection and power at the same time.

Farmers and domestic animals have lived and worked together for millennia, perhaps simply because it is much more enriching to live together than to live apart. The pleasure of the tie with animals is not only reserved for farmers, it is shared by all those who live with animals, and who are de facto small-scale farmers. Could we not consider that "pet" animals have a "service job" attached to their presence, just as animals living in zoos or animal parks do? The status of "farm animal" is today very hazy as a result of shifts in status between "wild" and "domestic", and shifts in the "domestic" group itself. This needs to be revisited, as we will see later.

Some farmers and pet owners seem to think that their separate relationships with animals belong in different fields, but I think there is only one real difference between them, and that is the place of death in the relationship. Some farmers are scornful of city-dwellers who put a bandana round their dog's necks, but do they not themselves put bells round the necks of their cows? Farmers talk to their cows and to their dogs just as city dwellers do, and farm dogs, for the most part, no longer have the difficult life their ancestors had.

I bred ewes, and from their part in the work, I drew an income that allowed me to live with them, appreciate their presence, share their pleasure in life, and surround myself with the sweet scent of their wool. I named, identified and vaccinated them. Like the majority of farmers of animals, I treated them when they were ill. I watched over their welfare by laying straw down in the sheep-pen every day, and checking the distribution of water. I took them out to pasture daily and I loved walking in their company. I talked to them, told them off and listened to them. I managed their reproduction. I killed and sold the lambs to whom the ewes had given birth, and this enabled me to prolong my relations with them. Today, I live in Paris; I no longer have ewes but I have a small dog. I have named, identified, vaccinated and sterilized her. I take care of her when she is sick. I watch over her welfare by checking her water bowl. I give her good quality food, and a comfortable mat. I walk her in the street every day, and when possible in the forest or the countryside, so that she can run and meet other dogs, and this walk is a shared pleasure. My income does not depend on her assistance in my work (although…), and this is why death is not an obligatory partner in our relationship.

The relationship that we maintain with domestic animals is, at its base, either a relationship of animal husbandry as farmer, or one where we live with an *animal "familier"/"de compagnie"*.[11] These terms which themselves designate the relationship with a dog, a cat or a hamster, refer to an affective field, shared by farmers and by owners of dogs and cats, and to the field of work. For many farmers, cows, goats and pigs are also "*familier*" animals. They belong to a family where the genealogy of humans and animals intersects. They are equally "*de compagnie*" as they are their owners' companions. They share their daily life.

Remember that in France more than one household in two has one or more "pet" animals. This is not just about feeding, caring for, protecting, rearing and controlling, but also for many, it is about reproducing, that is, inscribing an animal into a genealogy. Is this *to live with*? The fact that the relationship with the animal does not depend on the income it can bring in, and also the fact of only living with one or two animals, allows us to leave death out the relationship. We can leave it out on an individual level, but not the group level, as for each animal which comes into a household, how many die, or are put to sleep? Behind the small-scale farmers of pet animals, there are breeders of dogs, cats and birds, who live off their relationship with animals. It can also be noted that the market for pet animals is worldwide, and resembles in many ways that of farm animals. There are dog breeders, but there are also those who farm dogs industrially, as a product.

Thus, relations with "pet" animals can be similar to those with well-cared for farm animals but they can also be similar to those with animals who are less fortunate. In 2009, between 80,000 and 100,000 animals were abandoned in France. NGOs responsible for sheltering these animals, such as the *SPA*[12] and *Fondation Bardot*, have noticed that the numbers of

[11] Translator's note: companion animal. Both terms translate into English as "pet".

[12] Translator's note: *Société protectrice des animaux* (the society for the protection of animals).

abandoned animals has been increasing for a number of years. For these NGOs, the economic crisis and the financial difficulties of some owners can go some way towards explaining this situation, but it is above all pet shop sales of animals that is seen as the principal reason that owners are losing a sense of responsibility, because of the character of marketable object that an animal has in sales venues. The animal, with its microchip, passes over the till scanner in exactly the same way as a pair of boots do; they are easily bought, but equally easily thrown away, particularly during the summer holidays, when the animals become a burden. In certain members of society, this detachment, and this absence of a sense of responsibility in relationships with animals does not come out of nowhere. The main form relations with animals take today, which is only one possible model, is pitiless exploitation in the livestock industry, where, as we will see later, it is possible to process the massive slaughter of millions of animals for reasons that have much more to do with economics than with public health. In what way is a relationship with pets based on disregard and detachment which leads to abandoning them, and in many cases to euthanasia necessitated by the full capacity of the refuges, different from the same relationship with farm animals; a relationship which, in industrial livestock farms, is also based on contempt, detachment, abandonment and, worse than euthanasia, elimination?

Our relations with all domestic animals are one and the same, and there cannot be two weights, two measures of moral concerns regarding them. There cannot be obligatory respect for one group, and contempt accepted for the other, when both live in our company and are our responsibility.

For me, the problem as far as pets are concerned is that "small-scale" farmers of animals are not thought of collectively, nor do they think of themselves as farmers. The veterinary profession, faced with the relational incompetence of many pet owners, has acted on the problem and gives training, particularly in the education of dogs. Based on behavioural techniques, these training courses are probably useful and effective, but living with animals, feeding them, looking after them, asking them to guard the house, to be affectionate and available, to be present and sympathetic with the children, this is husbandry. Should this not also be taught?

Considering the relationship with pet animals as de facto, an animal husbandry relationship would help the general public to take stock of the challenges of sustaining animal husbandry in our society and of their responsibilities to domestic animals. Do the 600,000 visitors who come to pet and admire the animals at the Paris agricultural show know how threatened and fragile their tie with animals is? Large- and small-scale livestock farmers and breeders, we all have a responsibility towards domestic animals. We owe them an immense debt. I believe it is necessary to think about this together.

CHAPTER 2

Work and Freedom

Marx believed that work is the expression of human life (1846/1982). It is thanks to work that man transforms the world and constructs himself as a man, for first and foremost, he has to emancipate himself from enslavement relations with nature. Through work, he transforms this enslavement into exchange relations and negotiations. As humans, we forge our identity and our humanity through work as individual and collective action in the world, and work and amity together bring out the "best possible" in us, and in our relations with others.

Work and Emancipation

Animal husbandry is an archetypical example of this transformation. Human beings, through work, transform a predatory relationship with animals into a gift relationship, situated as we are between interest and disinterest, between constraints and liberty. This evolution is a factor in emancipation from nature but also in regard to individuals, both human and animal. Work performed with animals allows human beings to develop and express some of their competences in terms of inter-species communication, that is, through talking to animals in order to achieve difficult activities such as pulling, carrying, pushing, moving and protecting, or through seeing the world through their eyes. Work with humans allows animals to free themselves from their destiny as prey, to suffer less from

J. Porcher, *The Ethics of Animal Labor*,
DOI 10.1007/978-3-319-49070-0_2

hunger, thirst, cold and injuries, and to achieve unrealized potentialities. It allows them to enter into the human world and participate in human achievements. Thus, if life is hard, it is hard for men and for animals, but less hard for everyone than it would have been if they had not been together. It is thanks to work that something rather than nothing happens between animals and us, and a wonder of evolution that is rarely noted is our encounter with animals and the fact that we are capable of forming a society together. Remember that "domestic animal", does not refer to a small number of animals, but, in France, for example, to eight million dogs, nine million cats, seven million cows, one million goats and one point three million sows. Our society is as populated with animals as it is with humans, even if many of those animals have no place and are made invisible. Our society is populated, moreover, in a more distant and selective manner, and more often by means of images than by the real presence of animals close to us, by "wild" animals that we worry about, such as bears, whales, wolves and birds of prey.

For animals themselves, the "natural" environment is work. Farm animals live in two worlds: their own, of pig or cow, and the human world of work; the farmer equally lives in two worlds, his own, and that of his animals. For farmers, as for animals, husbandry aims at cohabiting in these two worlds in the most intelligent way possible, and it is this that allows work, for to work is to transform the world, it is to transform oneself, it is to increase one's potential, one's sensibilities and to emancipate oneself. Work in animal husbandry is a possible route to freedom for animals because it removes frontiers and calls for the gift and the counter-gift. It is freedom for them, or, if the work is distorted, it is alienation, as it is for us.

The place of animals in work, and thus in the human family, is difficult for some to envisage in terms of emancipation because "nature" in the form of "the planet", is very often thought of in positive, maternal and harmonious terms. All is for the best in the best of natural worlds, some may say. For farmers of animals, as we have seen, nature gives order to the world and is effectively all these things, but it is also violent, unjust and incomprehensible. "Nature" does not necessarily do things well. In "nature", trees grow and children die.[1] For farmers, it is necessary to respect nature and the natural order of things, but also to add sense, ties and sentiments to it by work. For animals, the good life is not a given, it is a promise of work.

[1] As Victor Hugo wrote in "*A Villequier*" (*Les Contemplations*).

Because *le travail* is firstly and necessarily experienced subjectively, the question of *du "travailler"*[2] is as important, if not more so, when considering the evolution of production systems, than when considering work itself. For Christophe Dejours, arguments concerning the notion of *"travail"* come up against an indisputable reality: *travailler*. The nominalization of the verb which takes us from the word "*travail*" to "*travailler*" is important because it stresses the irreducible place of the subject at work, we could say the *working subject*. *"Travailler* , or "working" has different rationalities and is not merely an economic rationality, to which it seems to be the most frequently reduced. "Working" participates in the construction of individual identity and of "living together" in society. It has a triple power: to transform the world, to objectify intelligence and to produce subjectivity" (Dejours 2009).

Occupational psychologists say that there is an irreducible gap between proscribed work through the procedures and organization of work, and real work, which is what workers grapple with. For the psychodynamics of work, work is to be found precisely in this gap: "Work is an activity deployed by men and women to respond to what is not already given in the proscribed organization of work." (Davezies 1993). The specific example of animal husbandry would allow us to apprehend this distance between proscribed and real work, and its consequences for individuals.

Since its origins rooted in the logic of industrial work, zootechnics, as shown above, has envisaged and constructed the work of farmers of animals as the application of procedures established upstream by technicians and researchers. Zootechnicians are "animal machine" engineers and procedure designers. Theoretically, a livestock farmer's work has been reduced to the execution of a series of chronological duties. Work, however, is never solely "execution", but always contains an element of "conception", of subjective investment, without which it would not be possible.

In the industrial system, animals such as cows and sows are "animal machines" and poultry and pigs are animal material, and must be treated accordingly, and looking at the work procedures applied to them, they are effectively machines or material; the reality of the way they are treated leaves no room to doubt this: male chicks from a breed only kept for their

[2] Translator's note: Both these words translate as work (n), so it is clearer here to leave the French. I will translate *travailler* as *working*, which to me stresses participation in work, and *travail* as work.

eggs are crushed, chickens are gathered up by vacuum pump,[3] young animals such as calves and piglets are repeatedly destroyed because of a glut on the market, and animals are destroyed for public health reasons, including BSE, Foot and Mouth Disease, Swine Fever and Bird Flu. For workers, however, who inevitably invest their affectivity in work, animals are still animals with which they have relations that go well beyond the theoretical definition of "animal machine". Despite prescribed procedures, workers summon this tie in order to work, and the work can be done because they do so. These days, however, the constant increase in industrial farming and the growing number of animals that farmers are in charge of has led to a growing detachment, even a quasi-rupture of the tie, precisely the rupture theorized by zootechnics. A large number of farmers thus find themselves with a big problem, even danger, as soon as they need to move the animals. To get round this "flaw in domestication", farm managements have put in place training courses on the handling of animals not just for new farmers, as was the case formerly, but for experienced workers. Put another way, the relationship between humans and animals in work, which zootechnics in theory, and the organization of work in practice, have aimed at eliminating, and which has in spite of everything continued out of sight for a long time, is now on the point of really being annihilated, and from accounts given by workers and in real work, the culture of animal husbandry is on the point of disappearing. The invisible persistence of the tie has for a long time allowed the theory to provide apparent proofs of its truth. Today, while the organization of work prevents relations more and more effectively, the theory, faced with an impasse, has borrowed one of its most significant elements from real work by reducing it to the status of a simple procedure: that relations with animals are not down to the subjective involvement of farmers in work, but are a learning process, as can be seen by injunctions such as "be a friend to your sows", and from ad hoc managerial selections.

This analysis does not only concern animal husbandry. As Richard Senett noted: "the modern work ethic stresses working as a team. It celebrates sensitivity towards others and calls for "soft skills", for example, knowing how to listen and cooperate. Above all, it privileges the capacity to adapt to circumstances" (Senett 2000, p. 139). But for Senett, this ethic is superficial, particularly because relations with time are degraded,

[3] See Jean-Jacques Rault's film, *Une nuit avec les ramasseurs de volailles* (a night with the poultry collectors) 2004.

and it is influenced by the sporting metaphor which impregnates group relations "in forms of flexible work, players develop the rules as they go along". (Senett 2000, p. 155). It is constructed on detachment and conceals "work without qualities".

Recognition of Work and the Tie Judgement

The question of recognition is topical in many fields of social ties (Honneth 2000; Caillé and Lazzeri 2009), and the search for recognition is without doubt one of the central questions in sociology (Caillé 2007a). While the animal condition is on the front pages of all the magazines and does not fail to mobilize intellectuals, the question of the recognition of domestic animals, meaning animals implicated in social relations, is not considered, for philosophers concerned with animals—and there are many of them as the market is buoyant—do not speak of *recognition*, because that implies *knowing* domestic animals, and in the main they do not know them. Recognition of an animal involves wondering about them and questioning them on their place, in order to give them a place, and this turns some theories on their heads.

For Dejours and the psychodynamics of work, work is central to the construction of identity and it is a factor in health. The positive impact of work on identity and subjectivity comes via a dynamic of recognition, for there is no work without someone who works, and the work of that individual must be recognized if work is to keep its promises. Work can increase sensitivity, allow individuals to flourish, or, on the contrary, crush them.

As is with financial recognition, work must have symbolic recognition. This symbolic recognition has two large fields of judgements: the judgement of beauty offered by peers, and the judgement of utility offered by those for whom the work is done, such as clients and users. Yet the majority of farmers of animals have a painful deficit of recognition. The beauty judgement has been made impossible by the intense competition between farmers, the utility judgement is very negative as farmers are very badly thought of by consumers, who accuse them of polluting, and of maltreating their animals, even though the French consume 26 million pigs processed each year by the livestock industry in France. It should be recognized, however, that consumers have no choice.

In the livestock industry, the "search for recognition" partially explains workers' adhesion to the model of work organization. The only possible route to recognition for livestock farmers is quantitative performance, and including them in the industrial sector imposes the criteria of evaluation. The "Golden pig Trophy" plays a leading role in this context. It serves to publically recognize the "best" farmers. Most of all it serves as a defensive "prop" against suffering and a "standard measure" for performance (Porcher 2009a).

Cooperation between workers is more based on confidence than on work contracts. Nothing, however, is written down. Cooperation cannot be imposed. Work can limit itself to prescribed work and to the particular interest of farm workers, and this trend is accepted in organizations, due to the spread of individual evaluation procedures to all sectors (Dejours 2003). This evaluation is made against the wishes of the workforce and at a cost to their health, even to their lives, for work is above all a place for meetings, exchanges and a realization of self through the recognition of others. If exchange is prevented, if mistrust replaces trust, if amorality becomes the norm, work loses its sense.

Trust is a prerequisite of cooperation; it represents the essential step in work ties of having confidence not only in colleagues but also in managers who one hopes will recognize each person's engagement in the business (Alter 2009). This confidence in managers amongst the workforce, inherited from the paternalistic practices of nineteenth-century bosses, has been perverted by current forms of liberal capitalism which no longer dress up domination relations with good sentiments. Thinking of work relations in the context of the gift, therefore, must not lead us to forget the inequalities of resources and capital at the root of the wage system and domination relations. Analyses of Bourdieu (1984; Bourdieu 2003) on this point are irreplaceable.

The psychodynamics of work, as the social sciences do more generally, does not offer a place for animals per se. They are in fact considered as machines and when I point out the strength of the tie that exists between farmers and animals, one of the replies most often given in discussions with sociological, psychological or anthropological colleagues is that there is also a strong tie between workers and their machines, that workers talk to their machines, and love them, as if the fact that an animal is alive, is the subject of its life and understands what is said to it, counts for nothing, and the only thing that is important is the idea that the worker gives to it.

Like sociology, and more specifically like the sociology of work, the psychodynamics of work does not avoid this distortion and this shows a conceptual void in the analysis of work with animals which is rooted in the theoretic foundations of psychodynamics, closely tied to psychoanalysis. Although psychoanalysis gives a vital place to the child in us, it puts forward a theory of the subject which obscures the fact that most human beings have lived with or live with animals, and therefore the child in us is very often a child with an animal, or on the contrary, a child without an animal. The ties farmers have had with animals in their childhood are described by them as constructive in their relationships with animals and their subjective relations with work. I have proposed the theory that, irrespective of which species, living with animals in childhood facilitates speaking the common cross-species language of intuition and the body with those animals that are the closest to us. I will take my own experience as an example, but I have heard dozens of farmers recount similar events: I was raised from birth with a cat. She features in most of the photos of my childhood and I have the feeling that she was always by my side, even though the fact is that she wandered off and led her life before coming in at night. I constructed myself as a human subject with this cat, and I have no doubt that it is thanks to her that I have a positive relationship with animals, with ewes, pigs and dogs. A part of my identity concerns the animal world (as well as the fact that my surname is the title of a profession with animals!),[4] and it was my friendship with the cat that gave me access to it.

If we do not take the place of animals in the construction of human subjectivity into account, we will miss important elements towards understanding our behaviour, for animals participate in our education. They teach us to speak wordlessly, to see the world through their eyes, derive pleasure from life and a thousand other things that should be recorded, although they are not always positive in their impact as they can potentially form a contradiction with the way of being in the human world such as is imposed on us by our human education.

This co-construction of subjectivity by animals is all the more important in work with them. How do we understand a farmer if we do not take into consideration the part of his identity that comes from "elsewhere", that he has "extra genes", as a farmer once told me? These "extra genes" can be understood figuratively, as a metaphor, but they could also be literal in a certain sense. I often ask myself, when observing the symbiosis which can exist between humans and animals and the reciprocal transformations which form our relations, if the whole part of DNA that biologists ignore, such as non-coding DNA, could be the as yet unacknowledged support

[4] *Porcher* translates as "Swineherd".

for our collusion with animals. As Donna Haraway (2010) observed following the work of Lynn Margulis,[5] "co-constitution and co-evolution are the norm, and not the exception, to domestic animal species". How can we understand, then, the relations between work, animals and death without taking that part of us which is animal into account?[6]

The place of animals in work and the inter-subjectivity of our relations have an impact on the recognition dynamic, as farmers and farm workers do not only wait for the recognition of their peers and their clients, they equally wait for the recognition of their animals, and the situation is more complex than it appears if we consider that animals also wait for recognition for their implication in work.

This is why I suggest adding another judgement that I have called the "tie judgement", to beauty and utility judgements for livestock farmers and workers. This is what workers receive from animals, and is therefore given by animals. We can make this judgement through the representation model—that workers *think* that they are judged by their animals, or in the reality model—that workers *are* judged by the animals. I prefer to make the second model the starting point in my research. I suggest that animals do not have a judgement on the results of work, as is the case in human recognition of work, but on the *means*. We can hypothesize, as we have to admit that we know nothing about it, that cows do not *produce* milk, sows do not *produce* piglets, but the work that concerns them employs certain means about which they can have a judgement, and this judgement particularly concerns the relationship with the farmer. This is why I have called this judgement a "tie judgement". The recognition expressed by the farmer in the context of this judgement is, for example, "My animals love me, I am quite sure", or "If animals could talk, they would scold us every day". In the first case, the farmer is recognized by the animals, in the second case, he is not, or at the very least, "it doesn't make him happy".

[5] Lynn Margulis is a biologist. She put forward the theory in the nineteen sixties, that complex cells with a nucleus and mitochondria were the product of a sort of fusion with more simple cells, with some large cells absorbing bacteria and integrating them into their organism. This symbiotic theory encountered fierce resistance at the time as it went against the dominant paradigm. Margulis put forward the theory that life resulted from association and mutual assistance, and not from competition.

[6] See also between animals, sex and death as seen in bull-fighting. Read the articles of Patrick Simeon, "*Miser sur l'intelligence du taureau*" (Bet on the intelligence of bulls) and Marie Frédérique Bacqué, "*La corrida entre pulsion de vie et pulsion de mort*" (Bull-fighting between the life instinct and the death instinct), in Porcher J. and Pereira C. (coord.), 2011, "*Toréer sans la mort?*" (Bull-fighting without death?). Editions Quae.

The tie judgement has therefore two dimensions, human and animal. The human dimension concerns the expectation of recognition from their animals ("They thank us"), and this judgement is as necessary as the others and participates just as much in the construction of people's identity. The animal dimension concerns animal collaboration in work. If they collaborate in work, a hypothesis that I defend and that we will return to later, they have in effect a need that goes beyond the limits of their "natural" needs and is not at all considered in industry, or in theories of "animal welfare", and this is a need for recognition.

Yet the new forms of human and animal resource management, very similar in that they have been reduced to short-term interest relations for humans, and dependence relations for animals, have brought about a levelling in human and animal conditions of life at work that reduces both to the status of "beasts of burden" (Porcher 2009a). In large industrial pig farms, the manager directs the production of farm workers and sows—which represent an important de facto workforce—at the same time. The implicit function of "director of animal resources" is in thought and function very close to that of director of human resources. Further, it can be understood very clearly that between "human resources" and "animal resources", the word "resources" is the one that counts the most to the management. As Marx wrote (1867/1994):

> In agriculture as in manufacture, the transformation of production under the sway of capital, means, at the same time, the martyrdom of the producer; the instrument of labour becomes the means of enslaving, exploiting, and impoverishing the labourer; the social combination and organization of labour-processes is turned into an organized mode of crushing out the workman's individual vitality, freedom, and independence.[7]

Social relations amongst humans, and social relations between humans and animals, are very close and can be analysed as mirror images. This is because work is at the heart of our relations with other humans and at the heart of our relations with animals. If we use an analytical methodology to consider the transformation of social relations from hunter societies to liberal capitalism, what are these industrial systems the consequence of? Did relations with animals start as being of a paternalistic capitalist type,

[7]Translator's note: From Das Capital, English citation at https://www.marxists.org/archive/marx/works/1867-c1/ch15.htm#S10.

and have they become liberal today? Can what I call "animal husbandry" be assimilated into animal relations of a paternalistic type, that is, exploitation disguised by good principles?

The anthropologist Richard Tapper (1994), as well as the sociologist Peter Dickens (1996), pointed out how much the relationship that we maintain with farm animals is tied to the production relations that we have with them, and how much these resemble production relations humans have with each other. Tapper proposes a theory of the evolution of relations between humans and animals on Marx's model: in hunter societies, animals share the same world as human beings, nature is not exterior to human society, community relations between humans and animals prevail; the first domestications, which saw animals introduced into the human dwelling, resembled slavery; pastoralism is a contractual relationship of a feudal type. With the livestock industry, we have entered into relations with animals of a capitalist type.

Our relations with animals are, therefore, for Tapper, intimately tied to the social and political historical context. Peter Dickens, supported by Barbara Noske (1989), points out for his part how much farm animals in industrial farms are implicated, like men, in a process of production constructed on the division of work. They too are "adapted" and they too are alienated. Dickens puts forward the theory that the radical division between the natural world and human society has facilitated the emergence of the livestock industry, which not only alienates animals, but also men, by depriving them of a mode of relationship that allows them to develop their own capacities. Marx stated that in transforming nature, we transform ourselves. Dickens asks, however, how we can think about this transformation if we do not know how we transform nature, if a more and more fragmentary division of work deprives us of an understanding of our effect on nature.

Tapper postulates that the process of domestication is purely an exploitation relationship, one of the enslavement of animals. This is the view held by the philosophers of "animal liberation", who compare racism with sexism and speciesism. If we consider that our work relations with animals are exploitative from their inception, and nothing more, the progression from slavery to the factory is inevitable.

It is surprising that these opinions are not accompanied by a reflection on work, for if there is a convergence of these two ideas, it would relate to work. A consideration of the question of work necessitates thinking of animals as something other than victims and natural or cultural idiots, who we must liberate in spite of themselves. The process of domestication has not been achieved without animals, but with them, and many species still remain resistant to domestication today, for are not certain species, such as wolves and bears, in the process of changing their status to ensure their survival? If animals collaborate in work, as I have hypothesized, then things are a lot more complicated than Tapper or the philosophers of animal liberation have suggested.

Tapper does not address peasant work relations with their animals before the insertion of animal husbandry into the capitalist world in the eighteenth and nineteenth centuries in France. These relations were not pastoral but were marked by strong proximity and the integration of the animals into the family. Can these be considered as paternalistic relations which later evolved into a relationship of an industrial type or "second spirit of capitalism" (Bolanski and Chiapello 1999)? In other words, does the family farm, which has already abandoned the values of ties with farm animals, now only think in terms of the techno-economic rationality of work?

Remember that animal husbandry is based in an asymmetrical relationship in which humans have real power over animals—the power of life and death—and this been accepted as such up until now. As we have seen, for farmers, this relationship is most often a coherent representation of the world and of nature, where the proximity between beings is compatible with their interdependencies and with the necessity for food. The relationship between humans and animals in farming concerns the family, affection, authority and respect in the same way as the paternalistic relationship between bosses and workers advocated by Le Play does. Certain rules of work that have changed in business have also changed in the livestock industry, for example, the idea of career. A worker used to spend his whole career in a business, and in a certain way, he was tied to it. Nowadays, this duration tie has been destroyed, as recurring unrest over the sacking of staff at insolvent businesses illustrates. The career of an animal—and this is the right term to describe the place of an animal in work for the duration—is equally a thing of the past. Cows are retired at five years of age, and sows at two and a half. The "career" of an animal is shaped by performance, and it ends when performance no longer conforms to the objectives.

But what is the model, and what does it represent? Remember that in the industrial society of the nineteenth century, there was profound inequality in status between individuals. For a noble or a member of the bourgeoisie, there were minimal differences between a peasant and his animals, or between a miner and the donkey that went down into the mine with him. Nineteenth-century literature, for example, Dickens and Zola, described the violence of the exploitation of men and animals. We could hypothesize that the paternalistic relations with workers was the result of a humanist movement which sought to distinguish between a worker and a beast of burden, meaning a beast of burden that was exploited by the capitalist, and not one that worked with a peasant, for the feeling of profound proximity with animals described by farmers today is without doubt close to the feeling eighteenth- and nineteenth-century peasants had for their animals. Peasants and animals lived together. In a peasant society, the relationship model with animals is the family model. As Keith Thomas pointed out:

> It is therefore perfectly true, as a seventeenth century observer contemptuously noted, that 'peasants and the poor distinguish very little between themselves and their beasts'. They go to the fields with them in the morning, break their backs working with them all day, and return home with them at night. Even their language expresses the affinity that exists between them and their animals, as many of their descriptive terms apply equally to both. Their children are kids, cubs or urchins, a little apprentice is a colt, and without thought, they use the same term for a puny child as they do for last of the litter (Thomas 1985, p. 125).[8]

While proximity relations between peasants and animals were based on the necessity of living and working together in order to survive, that is, forging a united front against nature, the paternalistic work relationship in capitalist society aimed at adding some relational and moral rationalities to the economic industrial rationality which, in terms of real work, were not there. From this last perspective, the issue of "animal welfare" belongs to a paternalistic approach, as we will see later. It aims to underplay the devastating effects of the exploitation of animals without questioning the industrialization of livestock farming, which is considered to be inevitable.

Animal husbandry, a nuisance we'd better do without?

"A new report from the Food and Agriculture Organization (FAO) affirms that livestock farming is one of the principal causes of the most pressing environmental problems, including global warming, land degradation,

[8] Translator's note: translated back from the French edition.

atmospheric and water pollution and the loss of biodiversity."[9] As the title "Livestock's long shadow"[10] suggests, the shadow beasts cast weighs the planet down; livestock farming could be a terrible menace to the environment. This was confirmed in 2008 in a publication by the delegation of Swedish left-wing parties in the European parliament (Holm and Jokka 2008) which stressed increasingly forcefully the harmful policy choices of the European Union, and in 2010, by a prospective publication which insisted on the environmental costs of livestock farming (Pelletier and Tyedmers 2010). Since then, a number of novels and essays, the "popular" press and many Internet sites have broadly echoed this institutional and scientific call to arms against livestock farming. What is the reproach against animal husbandry, "*Ce pelé, ce galeux d'où vient tout notre mal?*".[11]

According to these publications, livestock farming, or, much more particularly, farm animals contribute 18 percent of the greenhouse gas emissions tied to human activities. The finger is particularly pointed at ruminants for their CO_2 and methane emissions. At 33 percent, livestock farming occupies an undue proportion of arable land, and may help cause its degradation. It may monopolize water resources and pollute them. It may monopolize the biomass for its own profit. It may cause a reduction in biodiversity because farm animals occupy the terrain of wild animals. It monopolizes subsidies. Its energy efficiency is very mediocre as it takes ten times more energy to produce animal protein than vegetable protein.

What solutions do the authors of these publications offer to counteract this veritable plague? Bearing in mind that the worldwide demand for food is not going to stop increasing, and even in developing countries they are increasingly moving towards animal products, bearing in mind also that 80 percent of growth in livestock farms is taking place in industrial systems, FAO recommends more, and better industrialization. For

> There is a need to accept that the intensification and perhaps industrialization of livestock production is the inevitable long-term outcome of the structural change process that is ongoing for most of the sector. The key to making this process environmentally acceptable is facilitating the right loca-

[9] Livestock's long shadow. Environmental issues and options. Food and Agriculture Organization of the United Nations Rome, 2006 http://www.fao.org/docrep/010/a0701e/a0701e00.HTM.

[10] FAO magazine, Department of agriculture. Focus: the impact of livestock farming on the environment. November 2006 http://www.fao.org/ag/fr/magazine/0612sp1.htm.

[11] Translator's note: this is a quote from a La Fontaine fable, "*Des animaux malade a la peste*" (Animals stricken by the plague). It loosely translates as "This scabby, scurvy object, source of these bad events."

tion to enable waste recycling on cropland, and applying the right technology, especially in feeding and waste management.[12]

So "the environmental problems created by the livestock industry are not due to their large scale, nor to intensive farming, but mainly to their position and their geographic concentration".[13]

The aim in short is to support the direction taken by the intensive and industrial sectors who make the claim of High Environmental Worth farming,[14] in other words, standardized and certified "precision livestock farming" (Lokhorst and Groot Koerkamp 2009) applied through information technology and new technologies such as automatic milking systems, micro-chipping animals, remote electronic surveillance, precision feeding, building atmosphere surveillance, virtual fences, artificial insemination technologies and robotization. By these means "intensive ecological livestock farming" may be possible, and may guarantee food for the population of nine billion forecast for 2050. As for extensive livestock farms, it would be preferable to re-orientate them towards the service sector, In particular, in areas that are environmentally vulnerable, even though "taking a decision to move in that direction is complicated by the socio-cultural roles that livestock farming continues to play in many societies" .[15]

If FAO's report displays unambiguous support for the industrial sector, the report "Animal industries and climate", denounces precisely this livestock *industry* supported by the European Union. It does not, however, propose other alternatives except for vegetarianism: "The report's authors have come to the conclusion that large-scale conversion from meat to

[12] In Livestock long shadow. Environmental issues and options. Food and Agriculture Organization of the United Nations Rome, 2006 – Conclusion du rapport. http://www.fao.org/docrep/010/a0701e/a0701e00.HTM.

[13] FAO Magazine. Department of agriculture. Focus: The impact of the livestock industry on the environment http://www.fao.org/ag/fr/magazine/0612sp1.htm.

[14] We could speculate on the use of capital letters in the designation of concepts, as it seems evident that their main role is to make the words behind the initials disappear, because what follows after only ever makes reference to an acronym. Talk of *BEA* or *EEI* does not have the same consequences as talk of "*bien* être *animal*" (animal welfare) or "*élevage écologiquement intensif*" (ecologically intensive livestock farming). Note that this disappearance of words is an element in Orwell's "Newspeak".

[15] Livestock's long shadow. Environmental issues and options. Food and Agriculture Organization of the United Nations Rome, 2006 http://www.fao.org/docrep/010/a0701e/a0701e00.HTM – Conclusion of the report.

vegetables would mean major environmental benefits, even compared to meat from animals fed with locally grown crops."[16] Movements in favour of vegetarianism supported by celebrities such as Paul McCartney include the *"journée sans viande"*[17] (20th March) which is the French version of "The Great American Meatout", and a "Worldwide day for the abolition of meat", which are "for respecting animals, for the preservation of the planet, and for the improvement of health". These aim to achieve a day or week without meat, but without which meat? This is not a question that is asked.

The authors of the prospective study already cited (Pelletier and Tyedmers 2010) encourage drastically curbing the development of the livestock farming sector, and replacing it with the production and consumption of soya and poultry. The livestock farming that is blamed is overwhelmingly that of ruminants; the industrial farming of monogastric animals, in particular poultry, does not seem to present the same problems according to these writers. This assertion is quite surprising. Are not chickens livestock animals? Isn't industrial poultry farming just as disastrous to the environment, and to "animal welfare"?

These publications are very perplexing. First of all, as Simon Fairly, author of "Meat, a benign extravagance" noted, livestock farming and the consumption of meat certainly do not bear responsibility for the environmental problems that are attributed to them by defenders of the planet. For the author, the given statistics are not relevant and do not take into account the real activity of livestock farming as a method distinct from other enterprises, for example, the deforestation of the Amazonian rainforest, where the cause is not simply livestock farming. Incidentally, the supposed ratio in calories of one to ten in favour of vegetables leaves out the fact that if cows stopped eating grass, we would not eat it in their place. Contrary to the position held by many environmentalists, farming animals and eating their meat could be sustainable for the planet.

Basically, no doubt, part of the critical analysis by defenders of animals and the environment is just. Is animal husbandry, however, really to blame? If animal husbandry were really such a calamity, how could it have existed for ten thousand years and be consubstantial to the majority of human societies?

[16] The livestock industry and climate—EU makes bad worse, January 2008. A publication by the delegation of the Swedish left parties p. 26 – http://www.meatclimate.org/home.

[17] Translator's note: meat-free day.

Reading the charges, it seems that many of the points are really concerned with things other than *élevage*,[18] even though the term is popularly used and in a generic way, for example, "*élevage industriel*". Yet there is no **industrial** animal husbandry. The words are a contradiction in terms. Where there is industry, animal husbandry is no longer possible. Over and above problems of translation,[19] one can but notice that these publications refer to *the livestock Industry*, that is, to the worldwide industry for the production of animal matter. This industry does play a big part in the destruction of our environment, the destruction of livestock animals, and the impoverishment of millions of peasants around the world. And as Indira Gandhi pointed out, "are not poverty and need the greatest polluters?".[20]

The promotion of the industrialization of animal husbandry[21] and the confusion between husbandry and "the livestock industry" demonstrates the ignorance of many as to what animal husbandry is and what a farm animal is; indeed, farm animals are very little considered in any of these publications, except to be accused of emitting gases and eating gazelles' rations. Nothing is said about what constitutes the basis of work relations with farm animals, that is, the search for a tie. This is why nothing has been thought, nothing anticipated, of what is in the process of being lost on top of the vandalism of the environment. In the name of profit or in the name of farm animals themselves, animal husbandry, farmers of animals and farm animals are disappearing.

For livestock farmers themselves, the absence of collective discernment blurs the sense of work with that of profession. Until recently, farmers thought they knew what animal husbandry was, and what a farm animal was, even though they were not conceptualized as relations with real work. Since the nineteen fifties, they have worked to "feed the world", that is, feeding everyone was their mission and their pride. However, there is very little talk of feeding the world today, because despite the quantities

[18] Translator's note: This term is in fact translated into English in a variety of ways. See note 3.

[19] Most of the publications are in English and it is from British and US concepts that the discourses are built. See note 3.

[20] In 1972 at the UN conference on the environment in Stockholm.

[21] An FAO report published in 2009 downplayed this proposition and particularly highlighted the importance of livestock farming as a means of fighting poverty and food insecurity. The worldwide situation of food and agriculture. First part. The point of livestock farming. Organization of the United Nations for Food and Agriculture, Rome 2009.

produced by industrial agriculture, a billion people worldwide are still malnourished. The aim is now not to feed the world, but to feed the *solvent* world. Another reason is that although some have a mission to fill the corn and wheat silos, for others multi-functionality necessitates maintaining the space left empty by the disappearance of agricultural activities by accommodating tourists, by selling the "*terroir*",[22] the countryside and "nature", and by keeping grass in the meadows short now that cows are not there to do so. The profession of farmer is *en route* to "redefinition", but for a majority of farmers, it has lost all sense. The pollution of the planet, the public health crises which have led to the expeditious *eradication* of animals, the change in eating habits, the evolution of sensitivities, the eulogies to the great apes and to wolves, all this seems to be going in the same direction. Livestock farming is vilified in most of the press, on radio and on television, and consumers are being urged to "*végétaliser leur assiette*",[23] or in other words, to become vegetarian.

Yet farmers are consumers like any other. They are caught between relations with animals and food constructed by their profession, and the public discourse that eating animal products seriously damages the environment, health and animals themselves; breeding animals is therefore a clear case of speciesism, and killing the animals is a crime. It is because their profession seems to them now to be stripped of collective moral sense that one can meet vegetarian livestock farmers.

This paradoxical position demonstrates the power of relational and moral rationalities of work with animals, and at the same time, the necessity for these rationalities to accord with collective sensitivities. For what happens to the farmers? The problems they have are not with what they can control, that is, the daily life of working with animals, but with what they cannot, that is, animal transportation, conditions of slaughter, and above all, a sense of their profession.

In the field of industry, things are simpler. For many producers, *animal husbandry* does not exist. The livestock industry *is* husbandry, and this is all the more true as a great many producers, and, more particularly, their employees, do not come from a rural background, and do not know of a counter-model to industrial production any more than they know about animal husbandry from a historical point of view. Livestock farming, in

[22] Translator's note: this word carries the idea of the tradition, history, culture and produce specific to a region.

[23] Translator's note: a slogan that translates loosely as "veg up their diet".

their view, is the rational, modern, technical, competitive production of volumes of meat. Agricultural training and the sector management tell them repeatedly that what matters is industry. Everything else is no more than amateurism and archaism.

The image that the general public has of animal husbandry seems contradictory. There are on the one hand the showcases, for example, the *Salon International de l'Agriculture* (SIA)[24] which draws an annual six hundred thousand visitors, and on the other hand there is the representation of livestock farming given in the media. The image that the SIA gives amounts to a publicity communication,[25] because although the animals are real animals, and the visitors do not fail to pet them and photograph them next to their children, the representation that is given of livestock farming is absolutely fantastical. The "pig village" is a good example, as you can admire regional breeds of pigs (overall in France 2000 sows from the six remaining breeds),[26] when the reality of the pork industry (one point three million industrially-bred sows) is obscured. The media, on the other hand, shows the reality of the livestock industry, in particular, the violence against animals. Neither the SIA, nor the media, however, discuss animal husbandry. The general public no longer knows what husbandry is. Many do not know that each milk-producing cow must have a calf, and so drinking milk is indirectly eating veal or kid or lamb, or making others eat it. Many do not make the connection between the egg and the chicken. Yet eating eggs is *the same as* eating chicken. Lots of people consider themselves to be vegetarians while they consume eggs, milk and cheese. This misinformation and animal "liberators'" propaganda against animal husbandry has led to the growing promotion not only of vegan food, but also, as we will see later, of biotech food.

Most of the general public ignores what animal husbandry is, and what a farm animal is, and more generally, they also seem to ignore what a

[24] International Agricultural Show (in Paris).

[25] Note that when institutes and publicity agencies set up communication campaigns for the industry, extolling grass for cows, even though the aim is to accelerate the industrialization of dairy production, and that needs no pasturage, they say it is "the construction of a neutral argument, purely informative". Conversely, France Nature Environment has started a communication campaign stressing damage to humans and the environment from the livestock industry. It is a "scandal", a "shameful denigration", which needs to face justice.

[26] *Cul noir* pigs from Limousin (136 sows), *pie noir* pigs from the Pays basque (448 sows), Bayeux pigs (229 sows), Gascony pigs (871 sows), *Blancs de l'Ouest* pigs (115 sows), Corsican pigs (150 sows).

domestic animal is. Thus, dogs can be classed by some as "pets", without considering them, even so, as "domestic", consequently a domestic animal is a cow or a pig. For others, however, a cow can be "livestock", without being "domestic"; this term therefore designates dogs or cats for them. Wolves, bears, whales or wild boar are most usually considered as "wild", in spite of the fact that those who so designate them often pay them attention that is totally domestic: many of the animals are individually named (and naming animals, as Adam did, is an exercise in power as much as it is in responsibility), and electronically tagged. Wild boar and deer are today *reared* for hunting, without this enormous contradiction within relations with these animals being given a lot of thought.

Our relation with farm animals, and more generally, with domestic animals, is therefore very confused today. We could be satisfied with this, and leave the best world that we can hope for up to (almost) natural selection. Farm animals, and even animal husbandry is in the process of disappearing. Who cares?

The problem is that it seems that this disappearance is not much noticed, either by professionals, or by the general public. The loss is overlooked because we do not know what we are in the process of losing. Animal husbandry is not limited to producing meat or eggs, maintaining meadows or decrypting genomes. It is not limited to its productive rationality. Animal husbandry is an important part of our culture, an important part of our history: our common history of men and beasts. This history is not the property of the agricultural sector; it is a common good, and yet it is not taught in school. It is not taught at all. Why is animal husbandry not considered or theorized about?

There are many reasons that can explain this past and current lack of thought on animal husbandry; here are the ones that seem to me to be decisive:

- Until relatively recently, animal husbandry was profoundly imbedded in the peasant way of life, and thinking about husbandry outside the context of fundamental relations with life in peasant societies was difficult; relations with farm animals have for a long time been merged with agriculture's relations with nature. As Mendras wrote (1984), being a peasant was more of a condition than a profession, and husbandry has been a self-evident "natural" element or component of human ties with nature since the birth of agriculture. It wasn't considered necessary to categorize it outside of other agricultural work. It can be noted, incidentally, that the social demands made by peasants today cover husbandry without really distinguishing it from other demands; they distinguish between "peasants" and "farmers" and develop a criticism of the industrialization of agriculture similar to the one I make against the livestock industry in order to demonstrate its deadly character (Perez Victoria 2010). If, however, relations with animals are included in peasant work, they exceed the scope of it because of the particular challenges of relations with animals, their intersubjective character and the question of work that we are considering here. In my opinion it is necessary to conceptualize peasant work *and* to conceptualize the profession of livestock farmer as a social relation in the field of social sciences, as animals, unlike plants, have a subjective relationship with work.

- Published research rarely deals with the history of animal husbandry in France (Jussiau et al. 1999; Moriceau 2005), while it is easier to find histories of agriculture or the rural milieu (Malassis 1994; Malassis 2004; Roudart and Mazoyer 1997; Mayaud 2005). The mostly regional articles on the history of husbandry, whatever their interest; otherwise, give little space, if any, to work relations between humans and animals from the point of view of actors, and little place to the meaning of working with animals. Husbandry is described as an activity or system of activities, but is not thought of as social relations involving animals. It is described from the outside, that is, from the point of view of procedures, and not from inside. In this way it does not rest on a theory of husbandry which is not necessary to the description of the activity. The history of husbandry has also been considered from the perspective of archaeology (the beginning of animal husbandry in…), geography (Veyret 1951), anthropology (hunting and livestock farming, rituals of slaughter...) and genetics (Vissac 2002)
- Animal husbandry is essentially viewed from a utilitarian point of view, as is domestication; "men domesticated sheep for their wool…" This view still saturates the literature on domestication, starting with children's books. The analysis of relations between humans and animals is based on the notion of interest, even if the aporia of a real analysis is stressed by those who do it. Thus J.P. Digard (1990) argues that the process of domestication could not be explained a priori by interest that could benefit humans (milk, wool…), but nevertheless

defends the interest of power ("the megalomaniacal desire for possession") as the only explanation for the tie.

- From the middle of the nineteenth century, zootechnics imposed itself as *the* theory of livestock farming, exclusive of all thinking on work relationships with animals, and all historical perspective. Nevertheless, for some writers, zootechnics existed before the term was coined by Etienne-Pierre de Gasparin (1843–1848). What characterizes zootechnics, however, is less a scientific approach to animal husbandry which can be found before the nineteenth century, than a scientistic approach tied to an industrial, utilitarian and productivist model.
- The discipline of rural sociology, which could have been concerned with a theory of animal husbandry a priori, has never concerned itself with animals at all, and seldom with husbandry. Rural sociology studies the rural world and its transformations, particularly those tied to the "modernization" of agriculture, relations between the urban world and the rural world, and peasant societies (Alphandery and Sencébé 2009). It considers peasants and farmers, regions, biodiversity and the diverse forms of rurality in the world, but not animals. Rural life is constructed, and deconstructed, without them. Yet Peasant Studies[27] represent an enormous potential field of investigation, where a place for research into animals on a peasant farm could be found, as well as the process by which it has been transformed, relations with farmers, relations between animals in the rural world and their place in peasant work. It is a whole field of research that is completely untapped, and yet which today has immense interest and carries vital challenges for the rural world.
- Neither general sociology nor work sociology have shown any more interest in animals than work psychology has: on the contrary, they give a lot of attention to machines (Dodier 1995), and this is one of the problems with redefining animal husbandry in the field of social sciences, which unfailingly, when animals are under consideration, returns to the question of relationships with machines, as if basically everything has already been said, as if the inter-subjectivity of ties between humans and animals does not radically change the problem, as if thinking of animals in work from the point of view of sociology is impossible.

[27] In English in the original text.

- The domestic animal does not have a place in social ties, and there is therefore no need to think about this non-place. It is merchandise, an object, even though pet animals, and in particular, dogs, tend to acquire a different status. However, the act of differentiating our relationships with pet animals from those that we have with farm animals (Digard 2005) prevents us from considering the proximity of our relationships with both, as well as the fact that animal husbandry concerns them both and that both can be well or ill-treated. The utilitarian theory of domestication describes our relations with animals as purely a relationship of interest, when in fact we have relations which combine interest and disinterest and which we can think of in terms of the maussian gift with "pet" animals as well as "farm animals". (Mauss 1999/1923; Caillé 2002a).
- For the past thirty years in the West, and more specifically, in the last ten years, the philosophy of "animal liberation", whether declared as such or not, whether consciously or not, has imposed a moral position on relations with animals. These theories benefit from the absence of theories on animal husbandry, and even more so from the absence of a moral theory of animal husbandry. However, this is also an obstacle in the construction of such a theory, *construction* because an apparently indisputable value system has been imposed, and yet it is necessary to discuss it in-depth. (Mouret 2009). The developing field of Animal Studies,[28] as much abroad as in France, has been taken over by the ideology of "animal liberation", and this can be seen particularly in the attitude of the media. Farm animals do not exist in this field except as "animal as food",[29] as if the status of farm animal could be summed up by their becoming food. In France, the development of the field of Animal Studies, or indeed, which to my mind is preferable, of Human-animal Studies,[30] which takes into account the diversity of disciplines and their approaches and which would be able to give a place to farm animals, is still in its early stages.

[28] In English in the original text.
[29] As above.
[30] As above.

It could equally be that animal husbandry has not been conceptualized because it is not well known from the standpoint of real work—that is to say, by those who practice it subjectively, with their spirit and their body, as living work. It is with the aim of offering a more personal and embedded voice that I am connecting my professional journey and my personal experience of working in husbandry to more general research results, analyses and propositions.

CHAPTER 3

The Livestock Industry

Although my earliest research was on the subject of the affective relationship between farmers and animals or the love between humans and animals, and therefore on something very positive, the results of my research led me to think about suffering, and to begin researching it, as there seemed to me to be an urgent need to distinguish between animal husbandry and the livestock industry. To this end, I made the hypothesis that contrary to preconceived ideas on the subject, the livestock industry is not a logical step on from husbandry; rather, it has been developed in the margins of farming, but has come to occupy nearly the whole field of work relations with farm animals. In view of the fundamental differences between the two types of activity, making the terms distinct by not using the word "*élevage*"[1] when we refer to the industry, and vice versa, is an important consideration in the transformation of production systems, and for sustainable farming. My research into the livestock industry has focused particularly on the field of industrial pig farming as I was strongly motivated to interpret its ways of working, its deleterious effects and its probable progression, in part because I had been employed in this industry. I wanted to understand how and why this system endures, despite everything that makes it untenable economically, socially and morally. The business of industrial pig farming is also emblematic of the transformation of production systems because of the specific animal, as pigs are closer to

[1] Translator's note: This word is used in French for husbandry and farming.

J. Porcher, *The Ethics of Animal Labor*,
DOI 10.1007/978-3-319-49070-0_3

dogs than they are to chickens, and also because of the globalization of industrial pig farming.

It is necessary to define some concepts such as "Industrial Farming",[2] which is in current usage. "Industrial farming" does not exist; what do exist are industrial systems. As there is currently no definition of this concept, for the purposes of my research I have defined industrial systems as follows: "the group of activities concerned with the division of labour and specialisation, with the object of the large-scale exploitation of domestic animals, and the aim of transforming them into consumer goods with the best technical and financial results possible." One property of industrial systems is a great degree of delocalization, that is, not being too tied to any region or country, and no longer being "*paysan*".[3] The progressive delocalization of the poultry industry from Brittany to Brazil over the past ten years is an example of this. For industrial groups, if Brazil, Poland or China are more profitable than France, there is no reason to stay in France, for the production of poultry or pigs any more than for the production of jeans, shoes or computers. One large industrial group in Brittany consequently produces poultry in Brazil which it then imports back into France, largely to supply fast food businesses, at a cost that is one third lower than the same products produced in Brittany are. Benefitting from EU subsidies does the group no harm either.

Industrial systems must be distinguished, however, from intensive systems. A system can be intensive, market gardening for example, without being industrial. "Intensive farming" is characterized, not by specific production relations to animals, but by a process of intensification, for the most part borne by the land or through work. The current use of the term "intensive farming" to describe industrial systems is a shortcut which I believe we would be better avoiding. It would be more accurately termed "industrial systems" rather than "intensive farming" or "industrial farming".

"Making pork" does not refer to animal husbandry (breeding pigs), but to the production of the animal matter (*le minerai*)[4] which is characteristic

[2] Translator's note: The French text uses "*élevage*", with the sense of "husbandry" in this context, but I am translating it as here as "farming", as "industrial husbandry" is not used in English.

[3] Translator's note: Peasant—but carrying the implication of small-scale, locally produced and hands-on (the French word *Paysan* is derived from *pays,* which translates as "land").

[4] The term *"minerai"* (poultry, pork or meat *minerai*) is used in the agri-food industry to describe the volumes of deboned flesh that are used to make minced meat.

of "industry", defined as: "the group of economic activities that concern the exploitation of raw materials, energy sources and their transformation, and the transformation of semi-finished products into goods for production or consumption" (*Petit Robert*).[5] In other words, capital and labour are employed to extract and transform raw materials into consumer products, with the aim of clearing a profit. This industrial business of extraction and of animal production inserts the husbandry of animals into the process of meat industries de facto, in other words, it inserts the living into death. The farmer—or more accurately, the producer—within his cooperative, which is the true business, and is itself within the sector, is subject to the rules of industrial competition. Note that many pig farms these days are the property of investors and are managed by employees and not by farmers. In order to produce and sell pork in a way that is profitable and competitive, it is necessary to continually increase work productivity and cut costs in areas of production, first and foremost those of work, whilst simultaneously increasing the volumes of product. This is why "mega pig farms" (3000 to 6000 sows or more) and poultry plants have developed, where for as long as social and environmental conditions permit, very cheap labour is being used, for example, migrant workers in Spain. One can assume that, considering industrial pork production is the same worldwide right down to the organization of work, animal genetics, food and workers' profiles, the only difference for the consumer lies in what is said about the product.

In my different jobs, I learned a lot about how things work in agriculture, and I could connect some disparate elements, in particular, the violence towards animals and animal breeders, and more broadly, towards farmers. I also quickly became aware of the power agri-food companies have over our lives. While I was looking for temporary work, I answered an advertisement for an agricultural technician working on an experiment. At that time I had a BTS[6] and my training matched all the criteria required by the prospective employer. On receiving an unexplained rejection, I contacted the recruiter, who at first dismissed me without much explanation. When I insisted on one, after a discussion which eventually became friendly, I learned that the employer had rejected me because I was a woman and the work involved testing pesticides that could potentially have a negative effect on fertility. But, I asked him, what about men? His

[5] Translator's note: a popular single-volume French dictionary.

[6] Translator's note: *Brevet de Technician Superieur* (a tertiary two-year qualification).

answer was evasive, to say the least, but I understood the utilitarian logic behind the reasoning. The effects of this logic can be measured today.

Before I could take a BTS in "animal production", I worked for one season in a large seed company that experimented with hybrid varieties of maize, and while there I came to understand how farmers are manipulated, with what techniques of communication and with what objectives. I had already seen the link between dairy standards and the process of intensification during training whilst listening to milk industry managers boasting about how small-scale farmers were excluded thanks to the constraints which made these standards financially insupportable. When mixing with milk producers, I understood how violent the process is and how it is based on a desire for farming freedom and on a naive faith in progress and knowledge. Technicians were credible simply because they were technicians. They had passed to the other side—the side of those who knew. For me, coming as I did from inside the field of farming, as well as from a family of trade unionists, this naivety was surprising. A large percentage of farmers that I met had effectively no political analysis of their situation.

The power management has over farmers is not unconnected these representations. The pyramidal structure research and development have had since the 1950s has placed farmers in the position of receiving science and techniques, and effectively becoming "operators" themselves. Even if this conceptualization has been countered since, and farmers have been recognized as the originators of their profession, that is, as rational individuals ("farmers have reasons to do what they do"), the subjection relations one group has over the other remain. They are rooted in the political choices that were made to avoid collusion between workers and peasants by the Third Republic. In the world of work, "We will do everything to exclude peasants and integrate them into the model of land-owners—the bourgeois of the fields taking their revenge on the aristocracy are therefore the natural allies of the urban bourgeoisie" (Hervieu and Viard 2001, p. 43).

After the BTS and another period of work, I obtained a *Certificat de Spécialisation* (CS) in organic farming with the aim of finding work in that sector. I had done some organic market gardening when I was a farmer, and I wanted to learn more and then take up a job which accorded with my principals.

For the CS, I again worked on industrial pig farming because of my most recent work experience in industrial livestock farming and also because the agricultural school where the training was given had a "pig workshop" as revolting, if not more so, than the one I had left. The sows were held in near-darkness in a dirty shed and they were so tightly tied up that for some, the strap cut deeply into the skin. Visible pain gradually gave way to invisible suffering when the strap was forbidden and replaced by a cage.

I realized on that occasion, that considering the industrial violence against animals and the refusal of all agricultural actors, including those on the Organic CS, to face things as they really were, I had a moral choice between using force, and acting as certain animal rights groups do by throwing open the pig farms and "dismantling" them, for example, or using reason and the force of conviction. Hugo Latulipe, the director of the film "Bacon" (2001) also expressed this feeling of having been faced, in spite of himself, with a choice. He explained that he had directed "Bacon" first and foremost, "through necessity" and that, faced with the violence of the Canadian pork industry, he had had to choose between the camera and "terrorism". For my part, I chose the voice of reason because I did not only want to participate in bringing an end to this situation of violence against animals and against life, I also, and above all, wanted to understand it. I wanted to understand why the people who I knew in the sector, who were ordinary people, people to whom I felt close, accepted the violence and the senselessness of their work. What would it really cost them to say no? What is it that keeps this insupportable system going? More generally, why choose violence, disharmony and sorrow over generosity, harmony and pleasure?

While I was working as an organic inspector, another side of agriculture and farming was revealed. Not only could I meet farmers who practised animal husbandry again, and animals who were not mistreated, I could also, through discussions with farmers, analyse the critical motivations which drive organic farming and thus get a broader perspective on the changes that are underway. I clearly saw, however, in the inspection company where I was employed as well as during my organic CS, that from the management perspective (trainers or company directors), criticism of industrial farming was realist, and embedded in the capitalist system. Moral sense should not take precedence over administrative reason, subsidies and profits, and it is more desirable to avoid talking about sensitive subjects. The seeds of the industrialization of organic farming were, I think, sown with the choices made in those years, and a hiatus is already perceptible between organic farmers and their management in the search for legitimacy. The consequences of the choices appear in the scissions at work at the heart of organic farming today, between organic farming based in values, and industrial organic farming that responds to demands for better health and the protection of the environment, and which is ever more in the hands of the industrial sector and big distribution.

In regards to organic farming, we can only observe that the place of animals, as well as the question of work and more generally, the social question, is marginal to the preoccupations of its developers. Organic farming is becoming an industry modelled on "conventional agriculture". The conditions of life at work for workers and animals is a secondary concern (Herman 2008). Organic meat is promoted as "good for the environment" above being good for animals, and the criteria used to support the claim that the "good life is animals reared in organic farms" can be fallacious. Thus, the argument that "they grow at their own pace to produce quality meat" is at odds with the real-life expectancy of pigs or poultry; for pigs, as the age of slaughter is not usually different from in the industrial sector, as the organic sector uses industrial breeds that condition the age of slaughter; for poultry, because many can be found in very intensive conditions as their farmers are caught up in an organization of work that deprives them of autonomy.

Despite everything I was able to learn as a controller, I did not like the job and I wanted to do something besides inspect other people's work. This is why, when I learned that further training in agricultural engineering existed, I seized the opportunity and, after another temporary job in pig farming at the *Institut Technique du Porc* (ITP), I took the competitive entrance exams for a school for agricultural engineers.

I worked in one of ITP's experimental stations for six months. I asked the director to take me on, ignoring the areas of work done at this station, and what I could do there. I came at the right time and I was recruited on a fixed short-term contract as a technician in a team of four people—two engineers and two workers.

The station consisted of various different buildings where animals were fattened according to different experimental objectives. For example, I was responsible for monitoring animals in a building where manure was tested to see what happened to the food given to pigs. I distributed the feed to the animals, I washed the premises and I took samples. I assisted my colleagues in their buildings and I participated in different data collection.

After having worked in the pork industry in Brittany, I was not particularly surprised by the violence with which animals were managed. Yet the productive pressure was much lower at the station. The workers would have had the time to handle the animals without rushing, yet the rubber baton was still the favoured method of communication, and absolutely contrary to what seemed to me to be the most basic common sense, the workers moved the animals by entering the pen in front of them and shouting, before anything had happened to justify this behaviour. The inevitable result was that the pigs all rushed together into a corner of the pen and refused to move. Shouting and striking therefore became a legitimate means of moving them. In Brittany I had refused to hit the animals, and I also refused at the ITP. In "my" building, I applied the methods which seemed to me to be the best. I talked to the animals whilst working with them, I patiently moved them before weighing them or sending them to the abattoir, and I asked my colleagues to do the same when we worked in "my" building. The apparent disorder that was generated by my method of working—the animals were less afraid and therefore moved more freely when they left their pens—did at the beginning generate a lot of criticism, but little by little, something changed.

While working with my colleagues, watching them work and in discussions with them, I witnessed the importance of virility in relations with animals, and the denial of feelings. At the same time I came to understand how work relations with animals constructed the representations my colleagues made of pigs. They did not treat the animals as "stupid" because they thought that pigs were by nature stupid, but because the conditions of life that they imposed on them necessitated that they be stupid, and the only way of reasoning with stupidity was through violence. When I called "my" pigs "my *pépères*",[7] they mocked my "sentimentality", undoubtedly caused in their view by my being a woman, but at the end of six months I could observe that my approach to the animals had begun to influence my colleagues, although I was very careful not to point this out to them!

At the conclusion of this short-term contract, I signed up for a two-year engineering course at ENESAD.[8] It was during this training course that all the questions that I had asked myself began to find roots in a range of research and theories, particularly in sociology, because I discovered Bourdieu. I had read Marx, Politzer and others when I was young, but reading Bourdieu helped me to understand where I came from, where I was going, why I was driven by this search for (re)cognition, in other

[7] Translator's note: Affectionate "grandpa".

[8] Translator's note: Établissement National d'Enseignement Supérieur Agronomique de Dijon (National Agricultural Institution of Higher Education, Dijon).

words what I had done subjectively and socially, as an agent in my own life, by returning to education and applying so much energy to my studies. I could understand what symbolic violence was, and why peasants were collaborating in their own disappearance. Peasants are not "cultural idiots", any more than I am myself, but not being an idiot and knowing *more or less* what is happening is not enough to free them from domination and violence, because they have to work every day, and the domination and violence, that is, the subjection, has subjective advantages, when knowledge is more of a cost than anything else.

Symbolic violence has the terrible consequence of humiliating farmers and farm workers, and the burden on them is underestimated. They are burdened with the hierarchical organization of agricultural work, control having been inherited by technical science in agricultural businesses, the disproportionate place of administration in the organization of work, legal constraints and the red tape relative to land and herd management, whether for reasons of the environment or public health and the injunctions that constrain them to do or to not do this if they do not want to lose the bonuses and grants which represent an essential part of revenue for some farmers.

One concrete example of this humiliation is the resistance of certain sheep farmers to micro-chipping their ewes by providing the animals with an electronic chip (RFID),[9] which enables the animals to be followed and traced from birth to death. Traceability is supposed to go hand in hand with quality, health and security; the chip makes ear-tags and tattoos obsolete. However, many farmers are against chipping as it is of primary interest to the meat industry, and is of no use at all to them. For farmers, micro-chipping is a supplementary element of the optimization of the management, not only of animals, but also of their farmers. It can be assumed that in the event of an economic/public health "crisis", it will be simpler for managers to identify, control, quantify the slaughter and detect recalcitrant farmers.

This "electronisation of ewes", which has been obligatory since July 2010 on pain of being forbidden to sell, intensifies the feeling farmers have that they are no more than suppliers for the industry. Further, the reasons for their resistance illustrate that the control techniques that technical innovations facilitate apply to animals as well as to humans, and prefigure an Orwellian world. As Yannick Ogor wrote (2009, p. 166)

[9] Radio frequency identification, which uses the same sorts of microchips that are used in businesses and the transport industry.

> The changes brought about by radio chips are certainly not immediately evident, but they are enormous. It is the very nature of our work that is being obliterated by digitalizing ewes; it is the definitive victory of industry. We are no more than sub-contractors to abattoirs in the end. As simple suppliers of meat, we must, by means of the radio chips, guarantee provenance in order to better manage the potential risk to industry that we have become. If a number on a label has already facilitated our integration into the world of industry, it has not only been the fruit of industrial necessity, but is a facility that has always been used by farmers, whereas digitalisation is a purely industrial necessity, it has nothing to do with our lives.

It can also be noted that this "electronisation of ewes" is promoted by the administration and by the industry in the name of traceability, transparency and security. However, it seems that this method is, on the contrary, very falsifiable.

The "electronisation" of animals (both farm and pet, as cats and dogs are also chipped by vets) is not the only technical route to the development of traceability in the meat industry. For a decade businesses have tried hard to put retina recognition procedures in place for animals. As Stuart Ward, head of Optibrand for the European Union explains: "this technology is an easy and permanent means of identifying animals as the capturing of an unfalsifiable print of the vasculisation of an animal's retina is even more precise than finger prints". As with fingerprints, the retinal print is unique to each individual. "After an animal is identified one first time, it is easy to verify its identity some months or years later and to take an imprint of that retinal vascularisation to compare with a file of imprints already in stock. This cross-referencing of images is, moreover, computerised, and functions in a similar way to the files of human fingerprints compiled by the police." (Alteroche 2004). This retinal reading taken from a living animal would be equally possible from a dead animal at the abattoir.

These procedures, which have a clear place in the process of the industrialization of work with animals, purport to replace the tie with animals by digitalization, and impose a denial of the competences and aspirations of farmers and of many members of the public.

The resistance of many farmers to compulsory vaccinating against bluetongue has a similar cause. The bluetongue is a disease that is not transferable to humans, and against which the animals build a natural immunity. However, vaccinating against it has become compulsory, even though it has very negative effects, not only on the animals who may suffer miscarriages or even death, but also, in the long run, on consumers, due to the residues of toxic additives in the vaccine. If farmers refuse to vaccinate, they are forbidden from moving their animals seasonally, forbidden from selling and they suffer other different pressures. Farmer[10] and Consumer[11] groups have mobilized against this vaccination, which was imposed without any negotiation. As Daniel Bensaïd wrote: "The 'common good' is no longer only concerned with what nature is seen to have 'given free', in accordance with the classic arguments of natural law. From now on, it also concerns cooperative human production" (Bensaïd 2007, p. 74).

These tendencies are in complete opposition to the construction of sustainable farming. For, as the socialist William Morris remarked, updated by Serge Latouche (2011), a decent society is above all a society that does not humiliate its members. "The desire to escape contempt is a universal aspiration, perhaps the only true universal, and is only possible in decent societies. A decent world cannot be a world of material abundance, but it is a world without ugliness and without misery."

A Contagion of Suffering and Ethical Suffering

I believe that one of the most important contributions of my research has been demonstrating the suffering of workers in industrial pork production, and revealing the contagion of suffering between animals and workers. Suffering results in part from the physical demands of the work, but also, and much more so, from the violent content of the work.

The physical demands are tied to the dark farm buildings, the dirtiness of the work environment and the difficulties of working with animals in industrial conditions, including difficulties in handling the animals and tasks which oblige postures that are hard on the back or arms. Work in the industrial pig sector is associated with many occupational health problems. Problems for humans as well as for animals found in the livestock industry have common causes tied to living conditions at work in industrial and intensive systems, including enforced enclosure inside buildings, air fouled by gas and dust and stress and illness. Respiratory pathologies such as asthma and chronic bronchitis which effect animals and workers, including farmers and farm workers and also including

[10] http://www.collectif.org/ - http://gdrofco.free.fr/.
[11] http://www.atanka.com/actions/fco.aspx.

vets, are particularly associated with poultry and porcine systems. Pork production is also a particularly rich breeding-ground for the pathogenic agents brucella, streptococcus, flu viruses and Hepatitis E, which also affect both workers and animals. Potentially, the many viruses that develop in the livestock industry, and against which workers are powerless as the viral pressure is constant, could attack public health as soon as the viruses leave the production units. The first victims of influenza viruses tied with zoonosis, such as avian flu A/H7N7, AH5N1, swine flu and AH1N1, were workers in industrial pig and poultry farms, who to this day do not benefit from any particular protection even though the risk of a pandemic has been stressed by many experts. Moreover, epidemics of animal diseases have affective and moral consequences for workers, including a sense of culpability, the feeling of doing a morbid job and the feeling of betraying the animals through slaughtering the herd and being a pariah, along with the economic and public health consequences.

Production conditions and the extensive use of antibiotics in the livestock industry has created a favourable environment for the development of resistant bacteria, and owing to the modification of the sanitary environment, of the viruses that animals and workers are daily exposed to. It has been stated that the resistance to antibiotics that threatens the human health of farm workers and vets in the first instance is also a potential threat to public health. Pork industry workers in many countries are more often infected by the streptococcus aureus than the general public, particularly by the ST 398 strains, which are often multi-resistant to antibiotics. Six hundred and ninety-nine tons of antibiotics (with active pharmaceutical ingredients) are consumed in the French pig sector annually, and this is more than 55 percent of the entire quantity consumed by the livestock industry—1261 tons in 2007—or 237 mg/kg pounds of the equivalent live weight of the product. The tetracycline, sulfa drug, beta-lactam and macrolide families represent more than 80 percent of the tonnage of antibiotics sold, and tetracyclines alone represent half of all sold. More than 93 percent of the tonnage of antibiotics sold for veterinary use are given to farm animals, that is, to these products destined for human consumption.

In addition, the violent content of work acts against the affective implications of work which is necessary to ties at work. Affectivity is an irreducible component of our subjectivity and it is inevitably relevant in work. Animals are themselves subjective beings that are affective and that want to communicate, and work generates an inter-subjective relationship which workers must take into account. Although this is denied by the industrial organization of work which, following "animal welfare" scientists, reduces it to "interactions" at best, the affective part of work is very important, as has been shown by the results of my research (Porcher et al. 2004).

"Loving animals" is presented as an advantage in job descriptions for the sector, but in the reality of work, if we want to limit suffering, we should much rather *not* love animals. All my interviews have demonstrated that workers are constrained to not "have feelings". The only farmers who can "have feelings" are independent farmers who are financially secure enough.

In the livestock industry today, the economic-technical rationality of work is radically opposed to feelings. There are no exceptions, procedures cannot be adjusted. The choice of which animal to cull is "automatic" in industrial and intensive systems. The performance of animals is monitored by a computer and if it is found that they fail to meet their objectives, the programme will dictate that the animal is scrapped. This decision is imposed on workers as a technical necessity, as well as an appeal to "good sense", that is, "we cannot keep an animal that is not productive, that costs more than it brings in". Yet my interviews with non-industrial farmers showed that shared "good sense" is, on the contrary, concerned with feelings, that is to say, the understanding of giving to receive, and giving a second and perhaps a third chance to an animal. "Not having feelings" is not seen as desirable behaviour, but rather, a deficit tied to the organization of work.

It could be noted that monitoring performances, and the place that these performances have taken in the sense of work, is based in an extraordinary "addiction" to figures, which can be considered as the cornerstone of defensive strategies against suffering in the livestock production sector, particularly in the industrial sector (Porcher 2009b). The pig sector has produced a phenomenal quantity of figures since the 1970s, when a plan for the rationalization of production put in place figures intended to track accomplished work. These figures and the race for performance have in reality taken the place of sense at work. As Isabelle Sorente pointed out (2011), figures are a drug for us, we depend on them to survive, and the production of numbers ends up by passing as thought for us. For Isabelle Sorente, only the practice of compassion in its rational dimension—the dimension that allows us to distinguish between compassion and pity—will allow us to rediscover reason.

It is because feelings are excluded from work procedures that "technical slaughter", or the elimination of unproductive animals, has become banal. Day in, day out, workers must kill weak piglets, slaughter sows that are rejected by the abattoirs because they move with difficulty and slaughter boars that have "stalled", in other words, that do not follow the weight gain curve and remain underproductive. This deadly content to work poses moral problems for workers, problems that the pork industry addresses by denial.

Suffering is contagious between animals and workers because animals suffer, and because work relations with animals are inter-subjective. Animals are not inanimate work objects on which workers can act in all innocence. Workers are steeped in animal suffering, particularly as they are key players. It is they who seek out, jab ... and kill. It must be remembered that contrary to what is claimed by many "animal welfare" biologists and behaviourists, animals truly suffer, and they do not only suffer pain. This distinction is important, as reducing the meaning of "suffering" to "pain" is a way of forcing a denial of this suffering and by the same token, a denial of workers' suffering. The concept of pain is practical for biologists as they study animal biology, where hormones and other elements are quantifiable. The subjective animal, however, is unknown to them because like us, it cannot be reduced to biological parameters; if it were taken to pieces on the lab bench, it would tell us nothing. Robert Dantzer pointed out in 1979 that animals have a brain, and it is important today to take into consideration the fact that animals have subjective and affective relations at work, and consequently the concern is not only with pain, but more broadly, with suffering.

It is because work relations with animals are individualized that suffering can pass from animal to human—and, I have hypothesized, from human to animal, through empathy. (Porcher 2002b; de Waal 2010). When an employee checks for piglets in the uterus of hyper-productive sows for fear that they will die before birth, which they know causes pain, the sow surely suffers. She suffers from the pain caused by the check, incomprehension about her position in the situation, and uncertainty about what will happen. The worker suffers because the pig suffers and because of their own powerlessness to do other than what they are in the process of doing. The same applies when an employee must slaughter a sow with the aid of a mallet, or a matador when he inflicts electric shocks (Porcher and Tribondeau 2008).

It should be noted that humans, faced with suffering, put individual and collective defensive strategies in place (Dejours 1993). They construct a mental barrier, an armour that "shields" them. These defences stop suffering but they equally block thought; it is precisely because they stop thinking that they cease to suffer. Animals on the other hand do not have such defences a priori; they do not have the mental resources to protect themselves from suffering. Their life inside industrial buildings has no sense; they do not know why they are there or for how long. For a worker, the working day has an end, but for an animal, there is no end. There is nothing else. After the factory, there is no other life. The only exit from work is death.

When suffering in the livestock industry is under consideration, abattoirs are often brought up as an example of the difficulties of the work. Yet suffering in work at abattoirs or in production does not have the same cause.

While abattoirs are presented as the archetype of animal suffering that rightly concerns animal protection societies, human workers are either blamed or completely forgotten about, as they are in farming. Suffering at work in abattoirs effects workers in the "clean" sector differently from those in the "dirty" sector. As in industry, workers in the "clean" sector work with a material that they must divide into pieces. They do not see the living animal even if, although they do not see them, they obviously know that they were there, and that they arrived at the abattoir alive. Workers in the "dirty" sector, on the other hand, work with the animals. Transporters and handlers have daily relations of great proximity with animals.

However, unlike workers in the industry who are supposed to do farming but actually do something totally different, workers in abattoirs know that their work is death work. Strong work representations keep empathy and compassion for the animal at a distance. The workers kill to feed; they kill because someone has to kill. Industrial work conditions make it a nasty job, but this nasty job can be described. It involves work rhythms, the non-respect of rules, the consequences of intensification ("tired" cows whose udders still drip milk), or inversely, the intensification of work ("wild" animals that "have never seen anyone"). Work in abattoirs is of the order of a "dirty job" seen from the exterior but in the abattoir, for transporters and handlers, there is a legitimacy and a grandeur. It is, however, a very difficult profession and physically and mentally very punishing. Industrial work conditions have compromised this legitimacy and have increased the difficult drudgery of the work. If the work was hard 50 years ago—and we can have an idea of how hard it was by watching *The Blood of Animals* by Georges Franju—the difficulty and suffering of workers was limited by the collective force of the work. This is no longer the case today, thanks to the extreme taylorization of work.

The situation is different in industrial farming, where the workers can have the feeling of doing a nasty job, for example, by abstaining from consuming what they themselves produce, something that is much more frequent in the poultry farming industry than in industrial pig farming, but most of all they have the growing feeling of doing a *dirty job*, which is essentially that of eliminating the unproductive or underproductive animals which have been created by the industrial character of the work. It is moral dirty work. This dirty job cannot be delegated downwards, unlike in other sectors such as hospitals: owing to the shortage of workers in industrial pig farms, new recruits must be shielded to prevent them from leaving quickly. The dirty job is therefore performed by the management, contrary to what generally happens. It is only given to new employees—particularly women—gradually; it is presented at a certain point as a necessary part of working in a team (Porcher 2008; Mouret 2009).

Ethical suffering is defined as "suffering which is not the result of a wrong perpetrated against the subject, but results from committing acts through their work which reprove them morally" (Dejours 1998, p. 40). Ethical suffering in the pig farming industry lies in an absence of thought about the sense of working with animals. If "we produce pork in the same way that we produce shoes", what ethical rules apply to the work? Where are the limits between a shoe and a pig? In work procedures, there are none. Yet what of the workers who look at their pigs every day and know that pigs are not the same as shoes?

Ethical suffering in pig farms is caused by the fact of killing and by the conditions of this killing. It starts with killing piglets that have been brought into life because the objective of maximizing a sow's piglet production demands it. This piglet production is an essential measure for human and animal work productivity. In 1970, a sow had 16 piglets per year; the number is 28 today, and more than 30 for the "best farmers" who are awarded "golden pigs". This change has been caused by the drastic intensification of work, a reduction in the production cycle of sows and the just-in-time management of the animals.

The hyper-prolific sow which is genetically universal throughout the business gives birth to a large number of piglets (frequently 18 to 20, but often more), amongst which some are not viable. Employees must therefore kill them, and this they do by means of "*cloisonthérapie*",[12] which involves banging the piglet's head against the floor or wall, or hitting it on the head with a hammer. This elimination of piglets is systematic. It goes profoundly against the worker's desire to give life and save animals. It is the antithesis of "maternity" work, where the intention is to give life, and not to take it away.

Workers must also kill sows who are sick or lame, as the pigs will be refused by the abattoir if they are in a bad state of health, or if they have difficulty walking. The sector management offers tools and training that are supposed to make this death work bearable for workers. Although equipment such as CO^2 chambers to asphyxiate the piglets, electrocution chambers to kill the boars and power tools to electrocute the sows make it possible to avoid hands-on killing and to put a distance between workers and animals, the very existence of such equipment creates a profound uneasiness amongst workers.

This cadaver production necessitates the job of managing cadavers. Interviews we conducted in Quebec in 2005 before techniques such as composting animal bodies had been tried (they have been authorized since) allowed us to anticipate that would come to France: on one side the professionalism of in-house killing through ad hoc tools and the specialization of some workers, on the other side the rationalization of the management of cadavers and their disposal by incineration or composting. The recent privatization of the public service of rendering has resulted in an increase in the cost of collecting cadavers and in improvised responses from certain farmers in order to cut costs, by, for example, rotting the bodies on site or abandoning dead animals in the countryside. The pig sector is consequently keen to maintain control of this management in order to control costs. The chosen solution has been to ask the farmers to bear the costs themselves by requiring them to not only kill unproductive animals, a job that was previously performed by abattoirs, but also to manage their cadavers. These new tasks have therefore become the responsibility of the farmers and farm workers to whom they are delegated in a rational and logical manner, as if they were elements amongst others that are necessary to the competitiveness of the French pork industry. For if the fable of "family farming" has been abandoned at least internally, even if it still exists in publicity for the use

[12] Translator's note: this translates as something like "walling therapy", and is darkly ironic in intent.

of consumers, the pork industry in France presents itself as a family farm today anyway, and it is sufficient to look at the website for IFIP[13] for the farmers to see the truth of this.

This deadly development, which is a consequence of the pursuit of industrialization, also helps to accelerate it, for incinerating and composting equipment, like that used for manure treatment, is only economically viable for large organizations. Big businesses are therefore better able to make an environmental assessment than small ones. Composting cadavers is presented as a "natural", ecological activity, as the cadaver is no more than decomposing organic matter, just like vegetable waste (Mouret and Porcher 2007), but even if it is a logical technique for work procedures, for workers, the death work is unambiguously described as "disgusting".

This change in the pork industry, and more generally in the livestock industry, demonstrates a disturbing evolution in relations to life and a trivialization of dealing with the unproductive by elimination. The work in industrial pig farms has become, for one and all, death work, and is viewed as such by the sector, who aim at making both death (the compost from pig cadavers is spread on the fields, and the incineration produces energy which can be recuperated) and the living profitable. The system can finally be brought to work in a continuous loop: death produces energy to produce the living, which, when dead, will produce more energy ….

Although some pork sector managers seem to be aware of the particular slippery slope that production finds itself on, and pretend that we "must evolve the system from within", the sector in general does not show any signs of changing direction, on the contrary. Putting the domain of real work off-stage remains the rule. As the professional press demonstrates, work in pork production is seen as work without a subject.

The industrial system is cold, unfeeling, disaffected, violent, pitiless and cruel, but not the workers in the system a priori, the majority of whom attempt to resist desensitization. This is why it remains important for the sector to maintain the fiction of animal husbandry and "animal welfare" at its heart, for animal husbandry is a profession of care and of ties. However, when the fiction no longer stands up, the workers, as well as all of us who consent to the system, must face our own violence.

[13] French Pork and Pig Institute: http://en.ifip.asso.fr/.

A Powerful Analogy

> Sunday, Seoul has confirmed a further two cases of Foot and Mouth disease on a pig farm in the county of Bongwha in the south east, and in a cattle farm in the west-central county of Cheongwon. A record number of livestock—close to one point three million cows and pigs—have had to be slaughtered in around 40 towns and counties, or about 7 percent of the total livestock population, with a financial loss of eight hundred and ninety million dollars. More than sixty-eight thousand military personnel have been deployed in an attempt to halt the epidemic; President Lee Myung-Bak has called for "radical measures", in particular guaranteeing more vaccination. About one point five million cows and pigs have been vaccinated in a tentative and desperate attempt to contain the epidemic. There is a risk that the export embargo may be prolonged. Time is needed for a country to recover its world animal health organization non-contaminated status after vaccination is carried out. The South Korean minister for agriculture has indicated that about 1.2 million extra cows and pigs will be vaccinated in the coming weeks, and up to 6.5 million animals by the end of the month. Foot and mouth disease affects animals such as cattle, pigs, deer, goats and sheep. Earlier epidemic outbreaks in January and April 2010 led to the slaughter of around 50,000 animals. The authorities have decided to provide psychological support. The different trade associations involved in the massive slaughter of livestock in South Korea, which is experiencing an unprecedented Foot and Mouth epidemic, will be able to receive psychological support, the authorities indicated on Monday. The west of the South Chungcheong province has proposed stress management therapy for health officials, soldiers, police officers and farmers who have participated in the slaughter of more than ninety thousand heads of livestock so far in that region. 'We have heard of people who suffer from insomnia, panic attacks, hallucinations and a loss of appetite', said a government official from the province anonymously. In general, the most significant symptoms appear a month after the traumatic experience (…) 'We are attempting to convince them to seek psychological support as soon as possible', she added. 'This aid will be paid for by the authorities'.[14]

The European mass slaughter prompted by "mad cow disease", avian flu and foot and mouth disease, and the massive slaughter of three million "heads of livestock" (cattle, goats, sheep and pigs) in South Korea because of foot and mouth disease due to senseless escalation in February 2011,

[14] France 2. 10 January 2011. *Publication Info Santé.*

as well as five million poultry due to avian flu, confirms the disastrous state of our relations with farm animals and the fragility of those animals in the livestock industry. Remember that although foot and mouth disease is contagious amongst animals, it does not transmit to human beings. Moreover, public health policies other than the elimination of the animals could gradually stem the epidemic amongst animals. The problem is that this takes time. This massive slaughter is also, and perhaps above all, an economic slaughter; it concerns preserving exports. The means of mass destruction put in place testifies to this. In some cases, faced with the urgency demanded by the situation, some animals are buried alive in immense pits.[15]

This carnage has had a terrible effect on farmers. As we have seen, being a farmer is first and foremost about having a tie with animals, about feeling close and responsible. This slaughter, against which farmers cannot rise, and from which they absolutely cannot escape (as it is the military that organizes these procedures), causes terrible suffering and leads to sickness, even suicide. The fact that "psychological support" and stress management units have been offered to farmers and people tasked with this massive elimination, shows that the authorities are aware of the consequences of the destruction of mental health, and this support has the further objective of maintaining those affected so that they are able to do the "dirty work" which is required of them. It is indispensable for authorities that public health officials, soldiers, police and farmers can continue to work without too much collateral damage.

Those who were charged with the slaughter of animals at the time of "mad cow disease" also suffered anxiety and hallucinations. As Gaignard et Charron wrote (2005) following interviews with French veterinary technicians on the psychodynamics of work,

> in the end, the majority of participants affirmed a loss of sense to their work as they did not believe there was a sound scientific basis for the total slaughter, and this made the work more difficult to organize. It is more difficult to organize a task that you consider to be useless, expensive, above all when you think it is a duty that must be justified. All the participants described greater or lesser repercussions on their private lives from work related to

[15] According to a note from *France agricole* on 8 February 2011: "animals should ideally be killed, then buried in 4 to 5 metre deep holes, lined with 2 coats of vinyl. But this rule was ignored by necessity because of the quantity of cadavers needing to be buried."

> slaughter, including nightmares, insomnia, apprehension and feelings of guilt (…). The most striking for us was the use of vocabulary associated with Nazi methods.

This dramatic change really reflects the perception of many workers, and the analogy with Nazi camps, which in the early days of my research I mostly heard expressed by non-industrial farmers, is now used by a growing number of industrial farmers and farm workers themselves, not generally to reject it as outrageous, but to consider it as it is. The treatment of animals in the livestock industry has recently been compared to the death camps by Patterson (2008), who believes that farm animals are confronted by "an eternal Treblinka", not as an analogy, that is, as an approximation that helps thought, but as a rapprochement which inescapably leads to an unconditional condemnation of animal husbandry and the promotion of vegetarianism, as for Patterson, all work relations with animals are exploitation.

Analogy and comparison do not serve the same function in thought. I will define them respectively as follows: comparison demonstrates the similarities and differences between objects; it measures these similarities and differences, and weighs them in the balance. Analogy, on the other hand, is an imaginative exercise which brings objects thought of as very different a priori, closer together. Patterson makes a comparison that results in an equality. The comparison seeks to give answers and not to ask questions; farmers and farm employees, however, make an analogy. They do so because they do not understand what is happening, and they are trying to understand. This is also what Elisabeth de Fontenay attempts to do when discussing writers like Isaac Bashevis Singer, for whom "the scandal and the suffering of man has since the beginning been experienced in a shared a destiny and in a relationship of consanguinity with animals", and who believed that for the animals, "everywhere was Treblinka" (1998, p. 743).

The analogy then, rather than the comparison between industrial livestock farming systems which lead to the mass slaughter of millions of animals and the death camps, must not be dismissed because it is profoundly disturbing. It is disturbing, and it is precisely for this reason that we must confront it. We must confront it in order to understand what workers in the livestock industry confront, what farmers and those who are responsible for slaughter confront, but also what the general public must confront: the horror of these practices and logical conclusion that this analogy leads us to.

To better understand, I analysed this analogy of industrial systems with the death camps with particular reference to Primo Levi testimony (1987). He bore witness to the process of the animalization of man in the death camps. The "*Lager*,"[16] he wrote, is "a monstrous machine which makes beasts". As I showed in an article published in "Studies on death" (2002), the analogy with the death camps lies in an analogy with the system. The industrial processes in farming are part of a deconstruction. They endeavour to deconstruct animals, to de-animalize them and make them into things. The livestock industry is a monstrous machine that makes things.

The analogy with the camps made by workers rests on four major points: loss of identity and individuality, that is, mass processing of individuals, violence en masse, loss of communication and consent to death work:

1. The mass processing of animals has become more and more evident in time with the increase in e size of farms. In a farm with 800, 1000 or 3000 sows or more, births, losses and departures for the abattoir involve hundreds of animals at the same time. As all the animals come from the same genetic pool, their resemblance and their pink and denuded skin (selection has considerably reduced pig bristles), as well as the affective proximity between humans and pigs, cannot fail to bring to mind images of the movement of human crowds; the individual is lost in the masses. This feeling is exacerbated for farmers who go to the abattoir where there are thousands of pigs waiting;
2. The violence of the procedure for those who are confronted with animals in real work and the display of their own clean hands by those who decide the work procedures. This "banality of evil" is central to what Hannah Arendt portrays in her description of Eichmann as an ordinary civil servant, eager to respect orders and to stop the "needless suffering" of millions of people who he is accused of sending to their deaths (1997). As Primo Levi says, "it was simply a job, a job which was offered to him, and which he accepted." (Levi 1998, p. 242). Workers in pork production stress the disparity between the difficulties of their work and the calm assurance of the "gods", that is, the technicians or the directors of cooperatives. This

[16] Translator's footnote: a German word meaning "warehouse" that Levi uses to describe the concentration camps.

criticism is not however spoken outright, but communicated through the irony of the relations of force between workers and management.

3. The loss of communication is a key element in facilitating the industrial treatment of animals and it supports the analogy with the death camps; I can observe changes between the years 1990, 2000 and 2010 on this point. When I worked in pig farms in the 1990s, speaking to the animals was considered to be a feminine whim. Today, although farmers deserving of the name talk to their animals as they have always done, it can be observed in the livestock industry that the radio is turned up loud in the pig farms or the stabling because technicians encourage animals to be habituated to their producers, and the radio is the only contact tie they have with humans.
4. The consent to violence, and more broadly, to work procedures in industrial systems by some workers and by a large percentage of the management also serves the death camp analogy. The ideology is that obedience to orders is stronger than an individual's moral values, even though the risk to farm management, as indicated by Dejour, is not the same as the risk a soldier took by refusing to obey. Refusing to obey was death. This is not the case in the livestock industry.

We can add another element that has taken a particular aspect today, Orwell's *newspeak* from "1984", which is used by researchers, technicians and livestock industry vets. *Newspeak* serves to hide reality. Terms used include "*Soins aux Porcelets*",[17] which in fact involves mutilating the animals; even more seriously, "technical slaughter" is used to designate the elimination of unproductive animals; "rationalised farming" is used to describe industrial systems, (the term "rationalisation" has obscured the process of industrialization for a long time, and in a terrifying manner); "unit" is used to describe pigs or poultry.[18] Newspeak in the livestock industry uses economic and technical vocabulary, sporting vocabulary such as *the challenge, the race*, and *the performance*, and warfare (*enemies*

[17] Translator's note: literally, "piglet care", although it translates as "piglet processing" in English usage.

[18] For example, in a job advertisement describing an enterprise as "post-weaning and fattening workshop for 4000 units".

who are foreign rivals and *strategies*), the use of English,[19] and the prolific use of acronyms, figures, tables and graphics. As Orwell wrote in "1984" (1949/1984), *newspeak* is to prevent thought. One category of *newspeak* is therefore solely made up of scientific and technical words. A consideration of language as a tool for the derealization of work brings us to *Lingua Tertii Imperii* (LTA): the language of the conqueror, of the Third Reich, which has been analysed by the philologist Victor Klemperer (1996). The language of the conqueror is also used against farmers who seek to resist the industrialization of their profession, it is used to justify the mass graves of "mad cow disease" and these days the mass graves of foot and mouth disease; it is used again for the concentration of industrial farms that results in the disappearance of farmers themselves (inevitable "natural selection" put in train by the no less inevitable "capitalist direction of production"), and again for the obligatory use of a vaccine (against Bluetongue disease, for example), which causes an increased death rate amongst animals and despair amongst their farmers, who are caught between administration and concern for their animals, and who in the end have no other choice but disobedience.

Georges Bensoussan, who I asked to read my article before publishing it in "*Etudes sur la mort*"[20] (1998), and who encouraged me in this path, wrote in 1998 that the existence of death camps was not a "historical interlude", but is embedded in the rational process that is characteristic of our societies, a process which has western rationality and sensibilities concentrated at its heart, and which marks the "triumph of instrumental thought". The industrial system is an enterprise which aims at the deconstruction of animals and the construction of things. The process, however, does not work. Animals resist and persist in being animals and not things; it is *we* who lose our sensibility and our humanity.

It is difficult, it is true, to think individually and collectively in terms of this analogy, even more so as relations to Nazism is family history for all Europeans. How, can I, for my part, research an analogy with the death camps without thinking of my deported uncles? Of the one who died, Guy at Melk, and Leo, the one who returned and who I knew when I was too young to understand the "never again" in a text that he asked me to type, yet not too young to feel the suffering that he did not speak? At 17, I believed that things could be forgotten, and that my uncle would

[19] Translator's note: by French speakers.
[20] Translator's note: Studies on Death.

forget. I know today that 30 years after leaving the death camps, my uncle Léo, ID number 90176, had not forgotten anything at all. If he had lived another 30 years he would still not have forgotten. How then do I research this analogy, to enter into it, and not in the abstract, as if it did not concern me, as if I could consider it at a distance, objectively, only from the point view of workers? How can we not research it?

This question of work and the responsibility of sociology leads to a wider debate on the ties between critical pragmatic sociology. The recent works of Boltanski (2009) lead us to reflect on these ties from their foundations, and to dispense with simplistic oppositions. In my research, critical sociology comes first and is the foundation, and it is the starting point from where I can advance to other sociological approaches. It is comes first because it relates to my real work experience, that is, the choice of knowledge as a weapon against domination and violence, as I have explained above. It is tied, moreover, to the field itself. I think that as sociologists, we cannot *know how* the livestock industry works, and keep a distance. We cannot act as if it is our business to be "objective" and highlight political controversies. I am incidentally tempted to think that this is why the majority of philosophers and sociologists do not seek to really know, and stay calmly on the fence. Reality must not interfere with theory. Reality must not impede work. The livestock industry is a world of such violence that it even raises the question of whether it has any place at all in sociology and philosophy. As Bauman wrote, the question is less "what can sociology teach us about the holocaust?" than "what can the holocaust teach us about sociology?" "The analysis (by historians) demonstrates without a shadow of possible doubt that the holocaust was a window more than it was a picture nailed to the wall. By looking through this window we can glimpse many things that would otherwise be invisible, and the things that we see are of the greatest importance, not only for the perpetrators, the victims and the witnesses of the crime, but for all those who are alive today and wish to still be so tomorrow. What I saw through that window did not please me at all. But the more depressing the spectacle was, the more convinced I was that that those who refuse to see do so at their peril" (Bauman 2002, p. 11). What does the livestock industry teach us about our practices in sociology? What must we change in our methods in order to learn something about the livestock industry?

What industrial systems teach us about sociology is in my opinion this: we must take responsibility and see things as they are and not as we want them to be, that is, we must not refuse to look because we fear that we will see something that we do not like at all that goes against our theories. If workers make analogies between the camps and the industrial pig sector, what does this tell us about work, and about how we can know this work, make this work known, and participate in its transformation?

CHAPTER 4

Animal Death

In 1997, as part of a DEA,[1] I conducted some interviews in abattoirs on the subject of "animal welfare". My objective was to question the representations the transporters and handlers had of animals and of "animal welfare". To this end, I met 70 workers in five abattoirs in western France.

I did not know abattoirs; even as a farmer, I had never taken the animals there. I had my sheep slaughtered by a slaughterer on the farm and afterwards I cut up the carcasses myself.[2] It was in this way that I learned the fundamental difference between meat and the cadaver, and I am dismayed when "animal liberators" willingly confound the two when arguing that eating meat is eating a cadaver. In fact, excluding industrial systems, an animal carcass destined for consumption is never a cadaver in the sense of the representations that we have of cadavers and their biological destiny of decomposition or incineration. In a certain way in animal husbandry, a dead animal is a deceased being, someone who is dead, someone who "no longer functions because their body has ceased to function, but who still has an existence for those close to them (Larribe 2010)". The deceased have no place amongst the living but continue to be part of the social group, and it is all the more true for animals that it is thanks to the deceased that we exist. A dead animal, however, destined though they are

[1] Translator's note: equivalent to an M.Phil.

[2] Those that are only authorized by law for family consumption.

J. Porcher, *The Ethics of Animal Labor*,
DOI 10.1007/978-3-319-49070-0_4

for the butchers, must not be treated with indifference any more than a deceased person, and the bad job, the lack of respect for a dead animal which constrains workers in abattoirs, is one of the causes of suffering at work.

My animals were never afraid because I prepared the situation well before taking them to be slaughtered, or, for poultry, on the day when I killed them myself, so that they would feel surprise or fear. This was why my first encounter with an abattoir was a shock, not only as concerned the animals, but even more, and in a way that I had not expected, as concerned the workers. Industrial abattoirs are the nineteenth century; they are Dickens.

This research into abattoirs, which followed ten years after Noellie Vialles' anthropological research into meat (1987), produced new and very interesting results, particularly concerning the place of affectivity in work. Abattoir workers' relations with animals had not been studied up till then. The abattoir business was less reticent about exterior people coming inside than they are now and I could get a little closer to my desire of having great proximity to the workers while researching. I followed people in their work: transporters from the arrival of the lorry to the complete unloading of the animals; handlers, from the unloading of the animals to the place where they are stunned or until they were restrained. I watched people work and afterwards, I requested a moment to talk to them about their work with animals. The majority of workers agreed to talk to me as much as was possible, taking into account the constraints of the work timetable and the proximity of the foremen. It was in this way that I was able to understand very close up what it meant to unload a herd of pigs from a lorry in a minimum time, or manage the same pigs down the holding lane. Workers dealt with time constraints, terrified or surprised animals and repeated movements, to the deafening background noise of the immense factory that is an industrial abattoir.

Industrial Abattoirs: "Hard Times"

Marx wrote "it is not conscience that determines life, but life that determines conscience" (1846/1982, p. 51). The results of my research showed the decisive influence the organization of work has on the construction of representations and on work practices with animals. Transporters and handlers had a more positive representation of cows than of pigs, which was tied to farming conditions before the abattoir, and transport and slaughter conditions.

I demonstrated that transporters and handlers, in particular those who worked with cows, had an affective relationship with animals that you would not expect in an abattoir. This is why I gave a central place to the question of attachment in the analysis of these results. If abattoir workers "like the animals", as they said, how could they kill them while the majority of farmers could not? I showed that the difference lay on the individualization of attachment amongst farmers, but that the place of the "body" was as important for one group as it was for the other; "living with them", "being with them", "being amongst them" was a pleasure for transporters and handlers as well as for farmers.

Affectivity and therefore the "body" are very strongly engaged in work, and, therefore, it seemed to me that danger had a valorizing dimension at work, and I understood in the end why accidents, sometimes fatal, were part of the risks accepted by the profession. It is difficult to implement risk prevention policies without taking into account the affective and moral components of work. I felt that if I had been in the same position as those who worked with pigs, and had been put in the place of the transporters with the same time constraints, I would have been incapable of proceeding otherwise than they did. The same was true of the handlers, who had to handle pigs without brutality, that is, with the aid of a sort of plastic racket, but who nevertheless had to get 850 boars through the production line every hour.

The work of an abattoir, even though it is supported by the coherent justification that to eat meat, it is necessary for someone to kill, generates moral suffering through not saying, or saying badly, what an abattoir is, and through having work practices that go against the desires of the workers. The time constraints of the work pose a significant problem. As a pig-bleeder explained in an interview: "As for the pig, it is loaded onto the lorry quickly, transported quickly and killed quickly, because it is eaten quickly. That's it, in fact".[3] In this sense, the industrial abattoir follows the logic of industrial systems well. It is their business to produce and to kill en masse as quickly as possible.

Beyond the academic results of this research, this experience in abattoirs allowed me to understand that animal death is not straightforward for abattoir workers either but they must stick to the job nevertheless. Some transporters, for example, dissimulate about what they actually do

[3] I have calculated that after 24 years on the profession, this pig-bleeder had gutted between 6 and 9 million boars.

at work to those close to them. They have to make a living but also, once engaged in this work, to keep it meaningful.

I also saw the pressure abattoirs were under to produce animal matter that must be as profitable as possible, as quickly as possible. It is this which has caused the ceaseless increase in preparation work by farm workers before the abattoir, such as the refusal to accept lame animals which slow down the production line, and the demand for clean animals. These demands have a consequence for work in pig farms because, if abattoirs refuse to take animals with problems as we have seen, farmers are responsible for their elimination, and therefore there is a trend towards them being responsible for the management of their carcasses.

I also had the feeling, during the course of the interviews, that industrial abattoirs generate a heightened suffering for animals who had been well-reared. Pigs from industrial systems arriving at the abattoir do not radically change their environment. Industrial abattoirs are a logical step on from industrial farms. This is not the case for animals coming from organic farms or from farms which treat animals with respect. Once, while I was waiting for the arrival of a lorry in a large pig abattoir, I was watching the animals shut inside the access lane. On the incoming side, at the end of one of the lanes, a sow was sitting, looking at me too. Our eyes met and I read in hers such total tranquil incomprehension that I was more overwhelmed than I had ever been before. If I had not known that any such request would be inadmissible as no animal that enters into the abattoir can come out again alive, I would have asked to leave with that sow. I had the feeling that she did not come from an industrial farm, that she was there "by mistake", considering that the industrial abattoir itself is a gigantic mistake. Subsequently, I encountered "organic" animals in these abattoirs and I understood that "organic" or not, there are no alternatives to industrial abattoirs. During later interviews with farmers, I could measure how profoundly this absence of alternatives was a cause of moral suffering.

Changes in French law over the past 20 years have clearly favoured the processes of concentration and delegation. Abattoir workers express a feeling of losing the skills of their profession, as they have seen reduced to a series of divided-up tasks that are repetitive, and very often described as incompatible with the sense of a job well done. The meat industry is certainly not recent and Upton Sinclair wrote a description in "The Jungle" in 1906 that is as enlightening as it is tragic.

An extremely complete report (The Speed Kills You)[4] has recently been written by the Appleseed association in Nebraska on the subject of work conditions in the meat industry. It has been followed by a petition to the department of Agriculture: "Slow Down the Line". This action is interesting on different levels: first, it extends to meat industry workers the concern for welfare that had previously been reserved for animals. At the same time, it is ambiguous as it can be seen as an undertaking of work conditions, in the name perhaps of a clear conscience for consumers of meat. Considering that workers in the meat industry are very often foreigners who struggle to defend their rights, the fact that they receive outside support and benefit from a spokesperson is nevertheless a positive step. The step is also interesting because the social struggle relates to the business clients, and not, or not only, to the representations of workers themselves. The very negative flip side of this initiative is, like the claims of "animal welfare" in the industry, a reformist position which aims not to remove the production line and the industrial abattoir, but simply to ease the flow, and it therefore ultimately contributes to making the livestock industry socially acceptable.

Killing Animals

The death of farm animals is not an easy subject, and its importance as a scientific question is much underestimated. It is not attractive and many even think that it would be preferable not to talk about it at all. The death of farm animals is, however, the conceptual and practical crux of the issue of transforming farming systems and of the sustainability of farming. Thinking about the death of farm animals is, in effect, thinking about their life, for farm animals dying is no longer taken for granted. Even more seriously, it has become unthinkable, not only for many members of the general public, but also for farmers themselves, as some have become vegetarian. Farm animals' lives and deaths therefore no longer make sense, and have even become misinterpreted.

It is because men live with animals and animal and human societies coexist that animal death has changed from being an unanticipated event to being a premeditated event in the service of human life. Unlike game animals, in theory at least, farm animals are both partner and product of human work. Their ritualized death demonstrates their importance, but

[4]Translator's note: in English in the original text.

the sense of the death of farm animals has been obscured by the industrialization of farming. This is why it constitutes a central challenge in relations between men and farm animals in the industrialized countries and new negotiations must be made, as well as the reconstruction of farming systems themselves.

For zootechnics, the death of animals is not a problem. Animals are products or resources, and death is a necessary path to the transformation of the resource into edible goods, a detail in the process. If anthropologists do interest themselves in the death of animals, it is very often from the perspective of human representations and practices (Brisebarre 1998), and the central question is the eating of meat (Vialles 1987). Some historians have been interested in butchers and in abattoirs. At the beginning of the nineteenth century in France, animal protection associations sought to improve the fate of animals and the conditions of slaughter, and brought about a change in slaughter methods (Vincent 1997). During the same period abattoirs were moved to the outskirts of the towns out of view of the general public, and the majority of abattoirs today are designated by the name of the company which brings together the process of slaughter, cutting and transformation. The term "abattoir", as far as the large private abattoirs are concerned, is not mentioned on the road signs. I have heard tell during my interviews in abattoirs of an employee recently recruited to the accounting department of one of these businesses, who did not realize that he was working in an abattoir until a good ten days after he had started work.

Anthropological research into many societies illustrates how the slaughter of animals must be ritualized so that it can be accepted. From the subterfuges of the priests of Greek antiquity in causing the animal to give a gesture of assent to its sacrifice, to requests for pardon for Native American hunters, killing animals was never a simple inevitability. Yet since the Neanderthals (Pathou-Mathis 2006), who were great hunters and great consumers of meat, and Cro-magnon, the animal body has been an object of shared food. Anthropologists point out the necessity of affective distance from the slaughter of animals in the contemporary period, as in the case of pigs (Méchin 1992; Fabre Vassas 1994).

You can hear when listening to farmers talk today, how each one gives sense to the deaths of their animals and "ritualizes" them after their own fashion. "Feed the world"; give to eat and give to live is one shared justification. Note that for the farmers and abattoir workers that I met, the slaughter of animals does not amount to the "sacrifice" conceptualized by anthropologists, even though a range of rites can be put in place to give slaughter a spiritual dimension. It isn't necessary to think of the sacrifice in terms of the gift (Caillé 2000), but as the non-sacrifice, precisely because the sacred is absent from abattoirs. What is present for farmers is attachment, proximity, even family ties with the animals, and very often imagination and poetry.

Thus as we have seen, it is the gift of a good life which, for many farmers, legitimizes the death of animals and necessitates a "good death", that is to say, one that is respectful and dignified, but even this remains an ideal that they struggle to reach. The "good life" refers to the Maussian gift; it is not disinterested because the expected counter-gift is implication in work, and in the end, the death of the animal, or rather the animals, because we must consider the triple obligation of giving-receiving-returning from the point of view of a particular animal, and also from the point of view of the herd, that is, animal, as well as human genealogy (Vissac 2002).

For Louis Vincent Thomas (2000), as I said in "Death is not our profession" (2003), death is the ontological foundation of human society. Society only exists in and by death. Relations with death are an indicator of societies and a means of questioning and judging them. Thinking about death in a society involves thinking about the passage from life to death, defining the criteria for a "good death", and choosing a place for the dead amongst the living. These days it can be seen that in Western societies, where death is a powerful taboo, there is a movement towards a good death being defined as unconscious, painless, clean and quick. The criteria for this "good death" were very different in the middle ages or in the eighteenth century (Ariès 1975; Vovelle 1973). At the same time, there has been a tendency for the place of the dead to be more and more distant from the living. The dead have passed over fields, churchyards and cemeteries, to disappear into crematoriums, for today, perhaps more than ever before, decay has been banished. As L.V. Thomas wrote, "If death remains the worst of ruptures, it is precisely because it leaves behind a humiliating and repugnant cadaver: a symbol of absence, because the deceased has disappeared, and also a forewarning of coming decay" (Thomas 1980, p. 9). This decay is incompatible with the representations we have of a "perfect" body, beautiful, young, active and immortal. The denial of death in our society can be seen daily (Bacqué 2003). These days we mostly die in hospital, far from ordinary living people. This acts as a de-socialization of death, and we see its medicalization, its technicalization and the creation of a spatial and rational distance between ourselves and the dying.

Yet a consideration of death is important, because a consideration of death is a consideration of life. And if death has no sense, it is this lack of sense that gives sense to life, which confers on it its marvellous and precious character, for those who do not die, do not live. Death is certainly absurd, but not dying is even more absurd. A Jankelevitch said, it is more valuable to have a short but real life than to have an undefined existence which would be a perpetual death.

We don't know much about what relations different animal species have with death for their part. Do animals have the concept of death? Do they feel death? Do they fear it? What place does death have in their life? Certainly animals seem not to desire death any more than the majority of us do, and like us, they tend to preserve their life by fleeing from danger and resisting death. Contrary to what is affirmed a little hastily by certain writers, we ignore the question of if animals have a consciousness of death and are surprised "to be or not to be". Observing them seems to show that animals have pragmatic relations with the death of members of their species, which, incidentally, does not exclude them from recognized expressions of sadness in certain cases (Bekoff 2009). Recognizing death is verifying the absence of communication, movements and ties. The dead stay and the living herd moves on. Unlike human representations and religious constructions of death, it is evident that animals do not have a sense of an afterlife. There is no paradise for animals, and paradise is a place from which animals are absent (Baratay 1996). This is no doubt why the Galician Catholic church Sainte Rita in the 15th *arrondissement*[5] of Paris organizes Masses for animals, and offers blessings for them. Dogs, cats, rabbits and others have their own place in the church, to the great satisfaction of their owners.

If slaughter, that is to say killing animals, is the final destination of a farmer's work, death is not its goal; on the contrary, the wish of a great number of farmers is to be able to keep the animals for as long as possible. As with human death, the death of animals responds to a necessity, because, as L.V. Thomas wrote, life comes from life and therefore from death. Life with animals, and the relationship with death that this involves, rests on a certain relationship with the natural world and with time.

[5] Translator's note: Parisian district.

The decision to put an animal out of service, to slaughter an animal or animals is an event, something that happens, that has a beginning and an end, and this event is very often experienced as sad by farmers. For a great many of them, the abattoir is the "worst moment" of work. Although the hour of our own death remains unpredictable, even if, as it does with animals, we know it comes from outside—from bacteria, viruses, floods and earthquakes, a car coming at us, a radioactive cloud, war—we decide "when" animals die. Our foreknowledge of their deaths results in animals having the status of "being for death". They are the condemned on borrowed time, a status which is no more or less true for us. Although we know the day of their death, the animals themselves ignore it, even though the farmer gives off imperceptible signs, or there are some changes in the organization of work which might give them a glimpse of a change that concerns them.

Because of industrial changes in work relations with animals and transformations in non-industrial systems, the slaughter of animals has become a collective problem. Public rural abattoirs have closed one after the other in the name of European standardization. Farmers have found themselves constrained to delegate the transportation of their animals and their slaughter, to the industrial livestock industry, as regional abattoirs can be a long way from the farm. Small rural abattoirs allowed farmers to take the animals themselves and to discuss with the employees, for example, which animal should go before or after. It allowed farmers to take their animals "at the last minute", and to take them themselves. More generally, it allowed farmers to exercise their responsibility for the animals up to the abattoir door. This is why many farmers in different regions defend local abattoirs. Furthermore, it is worth noting that small rural abattoirs function like large abattoirs over the division of work, and are affected by the same legal constraints imposed by industrial procedures.

Many farmers and farmers' groups testify, however, that it is technically possible and economically viable to breed animals in a way that is different from industrial and intensive systems; for example, by organic and free-range farming and direct selling. However, the higher quality work experience of farmers using these methods is compromised in the end by an ethical and technical impasse caused by the lack of alternatives to the industrial organization of work for the transportation and slaughter of the animals. Whatever production system they come from, farm animals will be slaughtered, some compromises later, in the same abattoir, and transported there under the same conditions, via the same organization of work. This fact is a significant flaw in the coherence of systems, particularly in the organic sector, which claims to make ethically farmed high-quality products, while respecting the welfare of the animal.

For a large number of the general public, in particular for some animal rights and environmental activists, slaughter continues to be seen as farming's ultimate violence, and fundamental proof of the exploitation relations that farmers have with their animals: farm animals as being *made* for the butchers, and no rules can be respected in that domain, even though, as Sébastien Mouret (2009) demonstrated, farmers act from a moral sense based on the gift of a good life for their animals in their relations with their death.

To my mind, the current debate around halal and kosher ritual slaughter is a false one, especially as these procedures are conducted in industrial abattoirs. The belief that animal slaughter in this context can be ritualized is a mistake or a lie. When I asked abattoir workers about the difficulties they faced at work in the course of the interviews I conducted with them, the day of ritual slaughter emerged as a source of moral suffering, as workers' defences effectively rest on the belief that the animals do not suffer, and the "ritual" slaughter of animals, which involves having their throats cut without being anaesthetized first, makes the suffering obvious. This suffering is insupportable to many workers, particularly as it is devoid of any religious sense.

This explains why many consumers refuse to buy meat if there is a possibility that it is halal or kosher, which can happen because you can find halal meat, in particular lamb, which is not labelled as such in the aisles of supermarkets or at the butcher's. Those consumers, on the other hand, who do want to consume meat that comes from ritualized procedures, might find the acceptance without question of industrial rituals and the lack of debate on the subject surprising, as the only debate there is comes from the animal rights activists who oppose ritualized slaughter for religious reasons. Between the common understanding of anthropologists who do not risk anything by defending religious practices and demonstrating their legitimacy and respectability, and the animal rights supporters, farmers and abattoir workers who reject them, there is without doubt space for debate on the conditions for realizing truly ritualized slaughter. In my opinion, regardless of any specific religious requirement, the slaughter of farm animals must be "ritualized", because it gives a sense that transcends the practice of a worker in an abattoir. Killing an animal is not nothing, and it should be collectively remembered.

The slaughter of animals and the place of death in farming are very different depending on the production system; the place of death truly crystallizes the differences between animal husbandry and the livestock industry. It reveals the place given to life within systems, for "How creatures die is a key to understanding how they live—it is as if we cannot start to tell the story until we know how it ends" (Phillips 2002, p. 23).

CHAPTER 5

Living Without Life

What Purpose (and Who) Does "Animal Welfare" Serve?

In 1995, during some training that was a required component of my engineering course, I contacted some researchers from INRA[1] for my research into "animal welfare", an academic field of study that I was in the process of discovering, which seemed to me to be a possible approach to answering my questions on animal husbandry in the then contemporary context of "mad cow disease" and the attendant mass graves. I arrived at INRA seeking an answer to the question: "Is a farmer's affection for their animals a factor in the welfare of animals?" The first meetings with "animal welfare" researchers and the research that I did there was crucial to my subsequent research on more than one level.

I was innocent and full of enthusiasm, like the majority of students, but perhaps even more so as the questions that I was asking myself seemed to me to be something vital. I also had a very positive opinion of science and scientists, who I credited with intelligence and good sense. It was therefore with consternation that little by little I came to see my mistake. These scientists were completely cut off from the real world. They were supposed to be working on "animal welfare", but they knew neither farming, nor farmers nor farm animals. They only knew their

[1] Translator's note: French National Institute for Agricultural research.

J. Porcher, *The Ethics of Animal Labor*,
DOI 10.1007/978-3-319-49070-0_5

laboratory and the games that procured them experimental "*manips*"[2]: putting cows into a maze, making quails run on a carpet, mistreating animals in order to demonstrate their capacity for suffering or for having emotions. When I asked one of the researchers with which farmers he had set up one experiment that seemed to me to be particularly ridiculous, I was told "What farmers? But we don't need farmers, we have researchers!" Note well, all researchers: the contempt for farmers which was embodied in that response has not disappeared. It underlies all European legislation on "animal welfare", because the legislation is made by the same people, "scientists" in public life, animal rights activists in private life, and the zealous servants of the industrial sector, and in my opinion they are all the same as far as the animals are concerned. As farmers are largely absent from different research programmes, their results often demonstrate that there is no desire to work with farmers and their animals in transforming production systems; rather, there is a desire to impose "procedures" on them, to "teach" them, for them to "learn", to "guide" them, to "encourage" them, to "change their representations and their behaviour", all other things being equal.

The results of research into "animal welfare" carried out, for the most part, by researchers and students who are not familiar with either farming or farm animals, but with strongly-held theories, positions and great faith in their own good intentions, override the actual life experience of farmers and real work. The recommendations of these researchers in favour of "training" farmers and farm workers, rather than actually remedying the violence of the industrial organization at work, places the responsibility for this violence on the shoulders of the workers. In this way, industrial and disengaged relations with animals have been imposed on farmers for many decades, and now they are being reproached for the detachment that they are obliged to show, sometimes even by those who have contributed to the development of industrial agriculture. Researchers and technicians purport to teach farmers "good farming practices". Farmers' practical know-how has to a large extent been destroyed, and has been replaced by

[2] "*Manip*" is the term currently used in the laboratories to designate the "handling" part of the experiment. It is not uncommon for the organization of the "manip" to be put in place before the research question is asked, notably, for example, when it concerns comparing two items, such as equipment, animal races or living conditions. Thus, doctorial theses can be summarized as piles of "*manips*" without it being clear exactly what the doctorate is researching, what its framework is, and what the thesis is that directs all of this. (Translator's note: herewith translated into English as "experiment".)

something imposed by behavioural analysts who do not have ties to farm work. The farmer, like his animals, is seen as a vessel for scientific knowledge from whom researchers never seek what they themselves could learn, before presuming to teach.

This "real" science, which claims to be "objective", is based on a denial of the inter-subjectivity of ties between humans and animals. The affection between farmers and animals, which is my area of interest, is inaccessible in the experiments and reduced to positive or negative in the "interactions". The experiments have a further limitation that is equally great: the indispensable presence of the laboratory animal caretakers, the people whose job it is to handle the animals, and therefore do the de facto work of a farmer, even as, during the course of the experiment, they deny all the relational elements that are the basis of work in animal husbandry. These animal caretakers, on the contrary, can be detached from the animals and fail in their duty of care. Their function contains a doubly paradoxical injunction: to care for the animals and attend to their welfare and at the same time remain detached so that they do not influence the experiment. If the caretakers can, with a bit of effort, manage this double injunction, we know nothing of how, in their understanding of procedures, the animals integrate the relations they have with caretakers. For animals have a point of view on proceedings and on the people who put them in place, and excluding their point of view is the principle distortion of these experiments. There is also the animal's demonstrative desire to give pleasure that Vinciane Despret calls "the preference for accord", referring to interactionists (Despret 2009); in other words, animals have their own idea of what the researcher is looking for—a tendency that is very distinct in pigs—and animals can also act on their own initiative and therefore modify the gift.

This theoretical question of "animal welfare" rests on the idea that "welfare" is measurable and can therefore be reduced to statistics. This is why biologists and behaviourists working on this approach have been piling experiment on top of experiment for 20 years, and have accumulated detailed figures that are supposed to show the responses of animals to the questions they are asking. Yet on one hand, the questions asked by the researchers are not interesting to animals, and on the other, accumulating statistics does not amount to producing sense. As many farmers and farm workers have pointed out, after 20 years of funded research into "animal welfare", the conditions of animals in the livestock industry are worse than ever.

In the very dark novel "*Les Humains*"[3] (2000) , Stéphane Ferret (2000) imagined someone who, in order to understand what a man is, kidnaps one randomly, puts him in a cage and sets about observing him. The process drives the protagonists mad. Research into "animal welfare" also contains elements ripe with rationalist digressions, despite attempts to take animal lives in all their uniqueness into account. I am far from sharing Vinciane Despret's optimism when she speculates that animals are participating in transforming (French) scientists in a certain way, and that the scientists are moving towards "shared thinking" with the animals (Despret 2009). When research into "animal welfare" has the objective of conciliating "animal welfare" with productivity and the social acceptability of the industrial sector, there is very little opportunity for the viewpoint of animals to be seen. "Animal welfare" research is done without farm animals and without farmers, sometimes even *against* them, yet a farm animal is an animal with a farmer. It is not a farm animal on its own, and the pigs and cows used in experiments are experimental animals. Despite welfarists' presumption in generalizing the results to farming, there is no farming in their procedures and thus in their results.

"Animal Welfare" concerns animals by definition, and has done so since the development of the concept in the 1980s in France. At this time, industrial systems and the industrialization of agriculture had given rise to criticisms of the living conditions of animals (Damien et al. 1981; Dantzer and Mormede 1979); as well as this they gave rise to social criticisms, in particular, the effect of the process of modernization on human mental health (Salmona 1994b), and the economic legitimacy of systems (Colson 1980). These issues, however, were reduced to a consideration of the adaptability of animals to industrial systems and were taken in hand by biologists. Complex criticism of industrial systems was reduced to the question of "animal welfare". The question of work was removed, although it has boomeranged back during the last ten years, due in part to difficulties the workers have handling animals, and the shortage of workers in the industrial sector. The management of workers was put under the question of "animal welfare", and was considered in the same way as it was for animals: How could workers be adapted to industrial systems? (Hemsworth and Coleman 2010).

The danger of this development has been that "animal welfare" research is contributing to a greater degree than ever before to the spread

[3] Translator's note: The Humans.

of presupposed assumptions of applied ethology regarding human beings. However, non-explicit theories of socio-biology underlie this research (Sahlins 1980; Tort 1985) and these, along with a residual behaviourism, result in fearing the worst. In other words, these developments that I am criticizing are being taken as reality: in the livestock industry, workers and animals are in the same boat, that of the workers. There is a process of de-subjectivation in these systems, and this affects animals, who are reduced to matter; it also affects workers, who are reduced to their behaviour (Porcher 2009b).

I participated in an experiment which involved the "abattoir". The idea was to monitor if different treatment meted out to the animals, such as being kind or being indifferent, made any difference to the quality of the meat in the end. For reasons dating from my experience as a farmer, I did not think that my stereotyped behaviour during the experiments with animals could have any influence over the quality of the meat. However, I didn't know anything about it. This is why, despite my reservations but in the name of "science", I was led to drive the animals that I had in effect befriended to the abattoir, even to push them right up to the restrainer, and following this, passing from the side of the living to the side of the dead, to take samples of their corpses.

As I have said, I had been a farmer, I had killed animals in the context of my work and I think that the death of farm animals has a legitimacy that is based in a farmer's moral sense. However, driving domesticated animals to the abattoir in the name of science is a trial which does not lie in the moral field of animal husbandry. Killing domesticated animals, even animals that have only been socialized to a small degree as part of an experiment, is a task which, although it is delegated to some as an "ordinary" job at the abattoir, rests on a totally different system of justification. For workers in abattoirs, the killing of animals has a nutritional sense. We must eat and someone must kill the animals. What pose serious problems are the industrial conditions of the killing. For a trainee or for a worker in an experimental abattoir, the sole system of justification is science and the quest for knowledge. This is somewhat inadequate, and it is regrettable that moral questions tied to the work of killing experimental animals are so little studied or taken into account.

I therefore experienced great sadness at the killing of "my" pigs. The slaughter was carried out in a little multipurpose abattoir (Clermont-Ferrand). The workers agreed that I should drive the INRA pigs and that I should rejoin my colleagues afterwards to test the carcasses. On arriving on the "dead" side, I was hit by a chain that was circulating over the rails. I was struck on the brow and I found myself covered with blood, in the middle of the pigs, who were also bloody. Nevertheless I continued the tests with my colleagues. I will not do a psychoanalysis of the event, but this raw, shared bodily experience marked me profoundly. For this reason, in all my subsequent interviews, I was very attentive to marks that left suffering on the body, of wounds, of illnesses, of accidents which explained better than a person could do, the resistance to proscribed work and the feeling of sharing in the fate of the animals in a concrete or symbolic way.

This experimentation, and working in proximity with the welfarists at INRA ,was nevertheless valuable because it allowed me to understand both that I would not answer my questions with applied ethology as it is practised, and that "animal welfare" has an extremely strong political content which does not have the sense that I had supposed at all. The theoretical question of "animal welfare" does not seek to understand animals and provide tools for changing their lives, but rather it seeks to make their industrial exploitation socially acceptable, and to improve what can be improved without reversing the productivity of the systems, their competitiveness and their productivist ends. I have since been researching critiques of the question of "animal welfare" as it has been developed by French researchers in particular (Porcher 2005). The political and scientific consensus which backs this research issue is truly surprising, and merits real reflection.

Liberate Animals?

> I do not know where I stand. I seem to be completely at ease with people, I seem to have absolutely normal relations with them. Is it possible, I ask myself, that they are all complicit in a crime of such appalling proportions? Can all this be as I imagine it to be? I must be mad! But every day I see the proof of it. And those that I suspect even give me proof. They show it to me, they offer it to me. Corpses. Pieces of corpse which they have paid for with their money (Coetzee 2004, p. 156).

Elisabeth Costello's consternation as described in Coetzee's eponymous novel is shared by a growing number of the general public, who have lost any point of reference in relations with farm animals, and this has made them profoundly unhappy. Killing animals has become a crime; meat has become a "bit of corpse". These representations are an undeniable consequence of work procedures in industrial systems, in which animals are treated in a way that is morally insupportable for some people exercising their moral sense in consumer choices. There is also, however, an element of "animal liberation" ideology propaganda. Militants cheerfully organize actions which involve pieces of what purports to be human flesh being put in blister packs and furtively offered to consumers from the supermarket shelves. The message is clear: a cow, a pig, a human, it is all the same.

The "animal liberation" movement grew out of theories developed by Peter Singer in his seminal work "Animal Liberation", published in the USA in 1975, which can be very briefly summarized thus: Moral questions do not only concern humans, they must also be extended to animals, particularly, in reference to Bentham, because they can suffer. Conscience and sensibility must necessarily direct human beings towards an "anti-speciesist" position. The appropriation that we have had over animals since the beginning of domestication must stop. Animals must be liberated in the same way that the black community and women have been.

Nowadays for the most part, the liberation movement no longer bases itself on the theories of Peter Singer. The question of animal rights is an important part of the subject (Reagan 1985). Further, some animal rights activists distance themselves from Singer on the question of "animal welfare", that is to say the possibility of improving an animal's fate, and take a radically abolitionist position (Francione 2000). Moreover, the movement has a radical and active fringe in the Animal Liberation Front, where militants carry out actions aimed at attracting media coverage.

Moral philosophy is supposed to concern itself with the fate of animals. However, when Peter Sloderdijk (2000, 2003) notes that philosophical reflection seems to him to be ill-adapted to questions concerning relations between humans and animals, and then goes on to propose an analysis of domestication that is partial and incomplete (which suggests that he was right on the first point), he has highlighted a particularly sensitive aspect. Animal liberation theories are in fact singularly narrow (Porcher 2007). There is still the need to propose ethics for relations between human beings and animals.

One problem is that moral philosophy does not have the monopoly on ethical questions, in fact it leaves a great many in the margins (Williams 1990). Another problem is that "liberators" impose their moral position without any analysis of the real ties people have to their animals. Yet when it comes to animal husbandry, farmers *do* have a moral relationship with their animals despite the fact that in the end they take them to the abattoir. Work relations with animals are based on individual and collective values. The first of these values for farmers is the respect and recognition which is due to animals.

The concept of "animal liberation" is based on a profound misunderstanding of work relations with animals and therefore on simplistic domestication representations which are confused with domesticity relations, with animal husbandry and with the fact of eating meat. Philosophers and animal liberation activists do not in fact know animal husbandry. They speak in the name of animals, yet they have not been given any mandate from animals, and for the most part, they have not even met any. Their understanding of animal husbandry and relations with animals is limited to their rejection of industrial farming—which, incidentally, they only know indirectly—and by a false representation of work relations with animals.

"Animal liberation" is based on the myth of "liberation" and on a failure to recognize the differences between animal husbandry and the livestock industry. All relations with animals are thought of as an appropriation relationship which we must break. Domestication is described as a predatory domination model of the oppression of relations between humans, which is the source of slavery. This is why one part of the "animal liberation" movement associates itself with a libertarian trend.[4] But, as we will see later, this hope of freedom is an illusion. "Animal liberation" on the contrary, serves the interests of industrial agri-food and acts *against* the primary interest of animals, which is to exist.

One of the arguments most used by animal rights activists in order to stress the objectivity of their position is the denial of affectivity. Singer made this denial from the start of his work. It is not love for animals that guides the author, he writes, but moral reason: "Outside of this, as we have said, we were not particularly 'interested' in animals; neither I nor my wife have ever been particularly passionate about dogs, cats or horses as many people are. We do not 'love' animals" (Singer 1993, p. 10). We find this argument has recently been put forward by Jonathan S. Foer: "I do not particularly love animals, except for my dog, I have no particular passion for chickens or cows, but there are certain things that we must not do to them" (2011). This, to my mind, is really the problem. It is precisely because they do not *love* animals, that the question of love is not considered in their relations with animals, and that they are guided, like

[4] See the anti-speciesist site.

pure moral spirits, by ethics, that they can take these cold positions, which are apparently sensitive, but which are, in fact, disengaged. Unlike them, I love animals. I love my dog, and dogs in general. I love cows, chickens and pigs. I love animals, and it was for love, like thousands of farmers, that I took up farming.

This denial of affectivity is just as evident in the daily practical positions held by liberators. For there is the theory and then there is reality. In theory, Singer proposes "liberating animals". In practice, he provides McDonalds with (perhaps profitable) assistance in improving the fate of animals in industrial systems. This is also done, by the way, by the ethologist Temple Grandin, who also claims to work *for* animals by improving conditions in industrial slaughter.

We find this collusion between the agri-food industry and philosophies of "animal welfare" and "animal rights" on an even more troubling level in the ideas of the eminent philosopher Bernard Rollin, who is a professor at the university of Colorado, an invitee to many symposiums and public lectures on the animal question, and the author of several works on this theme. More prosaically and no doubt more lucratively, he is the cofounder of the business "Optibrand", which is developing a procedure for the retinal recognition of farm animals. Quite simply this concerns, as we have seen, improving the traceability of animals in the meat industry and thus helping the very exploitation of animals that he claims to condemn.

This, for some, demonstrates the concrete influence of philosophy in our daily life: Do not philosophers show that they are capable of developing the production processes for hamburger sellers? On the contrary, however, it seems to me that they prove their political shortsightedness at the very least, and at worst, how they have compromised themselves.

We have seen that improving the fate of animals while still keeping industrial work procedures in place is an impossible enterprise, as respecting animals is incompatible with industrial systems. In other words, Singer writes one thing and does another, as do Rollin and Foer. The latter asks "Should we eat animals?" and answers himself "no", because it is bad from an ethical point of view, given the way that they are treated. But he explains that "I myself am not completely consistent, I do not eat meat or fish but it happens that I eat eggs and drink milk" (Kaprielian 2011). Like many "vegetarians" who eat eggs and cheese, Foer does not act on his moral arguments opposing "carnivores". For what does he do in fact? He does not eat meat. But if he drinks milk without eating meat, it is thanks to other people eating meat, because you need cows and chickens to produce milk and eggs, and these animals finish their productive lives in the abattoir, and end up at the butcher's. The majority of meat bought in supermarkets comes from animals in the dairy industry. In other words, Foer can claim to have clean hands, because others take the dirty hands upon themselves. That is to say, they take upon themselves the complexities of life and death relations with animals, as we have seen.

What seems to me to be important is not to eat *less* meat in general, but to *stop* eating meat that comes from the livestock industry. Stop eating industrially produced meat and choose *farm*[5] produce. At the same time it is necessary to reduce our consumption of meat and animal products, for health reasons as well as for financial reasons, because small-scale farm products need to be more expensive, largely because of a much longer production cycle.

I believe therefore that not only does the philosophy of the liberators not help us to understand *how to live* with animals, contrary to what Singer claims (2004), they also do not help us to know how to live *without* them, if we take the liberators at their word and we "liberate" animals.

Many of us take the presence of domestic animals for granted, yet this is no longer a given, and may not be a given again. We could soon find that we are the only species in our society, that we are alone with ourselves, alone in front of our mirror. For after we have liberated cows, we must liberate dogs, cats and the hamsters. "No pets", proclaim the animal rights "advocates", and this direction is in keeping with the central thesis of "animal liberation". We cannot "liberate" cows and pigs and continue to "enslave" cats and dogs.

Strangely, Lévi-Strauss seemed to desire life without animals when imagining a future society where eating meat had almost disappeared. He wrote: "Agronomists will set about increasing the content of proteins in edible plants, chemists will work on producing industrial quantities of synthetic proteins (…) meat will only appear on the menu in exceptional circumstances. We will consume it with the same mixture of pious reverence and anxiety which, according to the travelers of antiquity, permeated the cannibal feasts of some peoples (…). This involved simultaneously communicating with ancestors and consuming, at their peril, the dangerous

[5] Translator's note: *Élevage* in the French text, with the implication here of small-scale and non-industrial (not necessarily organic) farming.

substance that had been the living beings who were or became enemies. Animal husbandry, no longer profitable, will have completely disappeared, so this meat, which will be available in luxury shops, will only come from hunting. Our former herds, left to their own devices, will be game like any other in a countryside made wild" (Lévi-Strauss 2001).

This text, late amongst his writings, and published at the time of the slaughter prompted by "mad cow disease", is cited by some as admirable, but in my opinion, putting aside the respect I must have for Lévi-Strauss, it is a text that not only demonstrates a complete misunderstanding of what animal husbandry is, but one which, while purporting to be opposed to the violence of the mass graves, proposes an equally monstrous and violent solution. This proposed change would effectively lead to the disappearance of farming. If the farmers cannot live by the sale of their products, they will disappear, and their rural function will be taken on by others. Lévi-Strauss's one little phrase "animal husbandry, no longer profitable, will completely disappear" is one of immense violence, because behind this disappearance of a profession, the disappearance of thousands of farmers and their animals is also intended, for how can Lévi-Strauss imagine that millions of farm animals could be "left to their own devices", made "wild", and become "game"? What does this mean? Unfortunately, what I understand this to mean is that wildness is preferable to socialization, abandonment to solicitude and fear to confidence. Farm animals would disappear along with their farmers, for there are no farm animals without farmers. A cow is only a farm animal if it has a relationship with a farmer, and a farmer of animals, without animals, is not a farmer of animals. I am not even sure if humans would remain *human* beings without animals.

The industrial treatment of animals by the livestock industry is a monstrosity, but the solution does not lie in the return to the wild such as the "liberation" of animals demanded by Lévi-Strauss is. On the contrary, this pseudo-liberation is an open door to alienation; it is placing ourselves in the power of the bio-industry; it is human beings narrowing their world to include just ourselves; it is the rupture of ties with animals without knowing anything yet of what the animals are capable of doing with us if we give them a real place. This pseudo-liberation is a return to the jungle and war against animals. We must defend the accomplishment of self and the discovery of our own potential that work in animal husbandry promises, and not condemn it in the name of its industrial avatar.

The Livestock Industry's Endgame: In Vitro Meat[6]

For both farmers and farm workers, the process of industrialization has brought about a profound transformation in work relations with animals. As they explain, the aim these days is to "produce at all costs, and at no matter what cost", not to produce animals, rather, tonnages of meat, pork rather than pigs, for what counts is the volume produced at the lowest possible food price. Work is surely organized to these ends in these "meat factories". "*Minerai*",[7] or animal matter, is extracted like coal from a mine. From the point of view of the industry, this animal production from animals is particularly arduous; indeed, animals are a curb to production because they are living, sentient, affective and communicative; they can fall ill, resist work and create attachments with workers. Because of animals, the production of animal matter is not as efficient as it could be. This is why it seems more and more logical to envisage bypassing animals, to attain animal production that is really modern, efficient, clean and potentially profitable, to have an economic activity—like others at last, as was the wish of the pioneers of zootechnics in the nineteenth century.

Indeed, the ultimate destination of the livestock industry is logically the industrial production of meat *without* animals, or what Lévi-Strauss calls "industrial quantities of synthetic proteins". It does not much matter in the end to industrialists if the processed meat used to make sausages, chicken nuggets and hamburgers comes from factories with animals, or without them. This is why the meat production that biologists have been working on for a decade is supported by agri-food manufacturers.

The process of in vitro meat involves taking some cells from an animal and multiplying them in a nutrient-rich substrate. As Jason Methany, director of New Harvest explains: "After the cells are multiplied, they are attached to a sponge-like 'scaffold' and soaked with nutrients. They may also be mechanically stretched to increase their size and protein content. The resulting cells can then be harvested, seasoned, cooked, and consumed as a boneless, processed meat, such as sausage, hamburger, or chicken nuggets."[8]

[6] I am summarizing here the following article: Porcher J., 2010. *Le stade ultime des productions animales: la viande* in-vitro. *La Revue Politique et Parlementaire. Europe : quelle PAC pour 2013*. n°1057. Oct–Nov 2010, pp. 97–104.

[7] Translator's note: This word is used in French to denote industrially processed raw meat. Its literal translation is "ore".

[8] http://www.new-harvest.org.

This production is also actively supported by animal rights activists, for, as was noted by an evangelist for vegetarianism, "In the 21 years I've been a vegetarian I have only 'converted' a handful of people. I have become more pragmatic over the years, realizing that if one angle isn't working, or isn't working fast enough, we must try others".[9] Thus, the American association PETA promised a million dollars to the scientific team, who by 2012, would "produce an in vitro chicken meat product that has a taste and texture indistinguishable from real chicken flesh to non-meat eaters and meat eaters alike".[10] "Fake" chicken meat that must have the taste of the real thing—does this mean the "real thing" that is produced in overcrowded intensive battery farms in 26 days? It must be remembered that this "real" chicken has almost nothing to do with meat. In the words of the producers (who do not consume what they produce themselves), "may as well eat the chicken feed directly". It is precisely because this chicken is not meat, but is what consumers are used to eating, that a move to in vitro meat will be even easier. Biologists are not in the business of actually producing meat, which would be difficult; they are working to produce a substitute which resembles what is already sold vacuum-packed in the supermarket aisles.

If the production of animal matter from animals has the problems cited above, it seems that the advantages of production of animal matter without animals are dazzling. That is at least what the biologists engaged in the development of this technology claim, particularly those within the in vitro meat consortium and New Harvest, which is an organization devoted to researching alternatives to meat that comes from animals.

First of all, in vitro meat would be good for the planet. If it replaced the living livestock industry, the production of in vitro meat would pollute less, reduce water consumption, reduce greenhouse gasses and produce only consumable products and therefore reduce the waste from cutting

[9] http://www.animalliberationfront.com/Practical/Health/Vegan-index.htm.

[10] "PETA is offering a $1 million prize to the participant able to make the first in vitro chicken meat and sell it to the public by June the 30th, 2012. The contestant must do both of the following: produce an in vitro chicken meat product that has a taste and texture indistinguishable from real chicken flesh to non-meat eaters and meat eaters alike ; manufacture the approved product in large enough quantities to be sold commercially and successfully sell it at a competitive price in at least 10 states. Judging of taste and texture will be performed by a panel of 10 PETA judges, who will sample the in vitro chicken prepared using a fried chicken recipe from Vegcooking.com. The in vitro chicken must get a score of at least 80 when evaluated in order to win the prize."

up carcasses. The diseases associated with the meat production (BSE), the quality of meat (antibiotic residues) and meat eating (overconsumption of fat) would be removed. There would be no more herds, no more abattoirs and no more contagious diseases. Those working in livestock farming would certainly lose their jobs but on the other hand, millions of jobs for technicians would be created in in vitro meat production factories (the promoters of this procedure do not say that all production could be easily automated and eventually delocalized). In vitro meat would offer an answer to the food demands of the nine billion humans expected in 2050, even more so as it is could be multiplied ad infinitum, and therefore would guarantee food security.

For consumers who are not sure about the idea of eating this "artificial meat", promoters affirm that the process is relatively close to the manufacture of yoghurt. It simply involves encouraging the multiplication of something that already exists in small quantities, in a favourable environment.

The most relevant advantage for animal rights activists is that in vitro meat would stop the deaths of millions of farm animals. As Odine Sherman from the organization "Voiceless" explains, "A lot of people might find in vitro meat icky—but then keeping animals in captivity and slaughtering them is pretty icky too. For people who like meat—but not how it's produced—it could be a viable alternative."

In vitro meat as part of our nutrition is not science fiction in the current biotechnical environment. Following from genetically modified crops, GMO animals and cloned animals are nearly on our plates already. The billions of benefits at play in these developments outweigh without doubt any other consideration. This is why it is credible that in vitro meat will also be on our plates in a decade.

It is, however, surprising how little controversy this innovation is giving rise to. If some have noticed that the energy costs necessary for running in vitro meat factories would be very high, and others, that the development of this technology would hurt small-scale farms as well as large-scale ones, the arguments for animal husbandry as an alternative to in vitro meat have not been developed. Some animal rights activists are concerned about how we would be able to tell the difference between "real" and false chicken, but is the "real" chicken in question one that actually comes from poultry production units,[11] or does it come from an animal that has been

[11] These production units contain tens of thousands of animals, often designated as "pieces".

bred with dignity by a farmer? The answer is unambiguous; producing for fast food and mass consumption is the top priority.

It is also surprising to note up to what point animal rights activists and industrialists are objectively allied *against* animals (Porcher 2007). This is hardly a scoop regarding industrialists, who, as I have said earlier, have no interest in burdening themselves with this immense animal workforce (Porcher 2008), but it is definitely strange in the case of animal rights defenders. For where do criticism of farming (and not just industrial farming) and the promotion of in vitro meat take us, if not to a break with farm animals? Why is there this shared desire to get rid of animals?

The de facto alliance of industrialists and animal rights activists is the result of a common vision of modernity as a wrenching away from nature. For industrialists it concerns reaching the maximum mastery of technology, independent of the environment and therefore without affecting it: pure production that leaves no mark. It is about being morally pure and clean by not participating in the killing of animals.[12] This is why the quest for purity is associated with a hygienist view which seeks to distance itself from sickness and suffering, and from the disposal of anything that is impure. Indeed, we can witness that this search for purity leads to a preference for the industrial "living", over life, that is to say, living *without* life.

This industrial development, in spite of questions as to its technical feasibility on a grand scale, is all the more probable as it has the blessing of both industrialists and animal rights activists, the latter of whom are already busy promoting it to consumers in a way that industrialists would without doubt fail to do equally convincingly.

This sad picture, which is reminiscent of the science fiction plot of Richard Fleischer's "Soylent Green" (1974), must be taken seriously because it is supported by two opposing fantasies that the power of technology can make reality: the fantasy of absolute power, the fantasy of a world without violence or death, the fantasy of a human world that is above nature, and thus the symbol of ecological purity is "vertical agriculture": an urban skyscraper which would be able to produce in vitro meat and vegetables grown in an off-ground cultivation system, in a closed loop.

[12] This concerns feeding dogs and cats. In vitro meat is a moral godsend for animal rights activists who also want to feed their pets without having to face moral contradictions and dietary impasses (cats and dogs are carnivores), or biotechnological challenges (making dogs and cats vegetarian through genetic manipulation).

Yet what in vitro meat factories would be producing is living death, just as the livestock industry deals with life—the life of animals—for the production of animal matter. The animals are not alive, they are living, biological matter to be transformed. This is why inside an industrial abattoir, the procedure for killing is just one element between upstream (industrial production) and downstream (transformation and distribution).

It is living because it involves living cells in the biological meaning of the term, but it is also dead because it has no relations with a subjective life, a life lived, a sentient life, an affective life. The production of in vitro meat is the triumph of the technical without subject, the destruction of culture and the regression of ways of accomplishing life that Michel Henry calls barbarity (1987). In the name of profit and in the name of compassion, our future resembles a world of zombies.

We must live to die, wrote Jankélévitch. The difference between meat that comes from an animal and in vitro meat is precisely that: life. Life circulates between animals and us, life and death are given; we know, however, from whence our living energy comes. It comes from this incorporation of life by giving death. In the case of in vitro meat, there is no death, but there is no life. Nothing circulates, not life, not death, no gift; living death.

CHAPTER 6

Living with Animals: A Utopia for the Twenty-First Century

This is the point we have reached in our relations with farm animals. On one side there is the livestock industry and its collateral damage: the mass graves; on the other side, there are the industrialists and animal rights activists who are working in tandem towards the disappearance of domestic animals. Between the two, there are bewildered farmers of animals, the general public and the animals themselves, of whom no one is asking the opinion.

Animal husbandry is disappearing, in terms of work relations with domestic animals. This is not only a concern for farmers and for lovers of cows, pigs and sheep, but also for the owners of dogs, cats or rabbits. For what is at issue are domestic relationships with animals, or the insertion of animals into the human *domus*. After having lived 10,000 years with animals, we are putting a social world in place from which they are excluded, not because this is what we really want collectively, but because this seems to be the most reasonable direction, the most realistic in the context of the utilitarian thought that motivates us. What is the good of farm animals if animal products can be replaced by vegetable and biotechnical products? What good are dogs and cats if they can be replaced by robots?

What makes the difference, as we have seen, is the relationship with life and death. It is our capacity to enter into the world of animals and to change our point of view. For living with animals transforms us; animals educate us and give us skills that we ourselves think were lacking. Living

J. Porcher, *The Ethics of Animal Labor*,
DOI 10.1007/978-3-319-49070-0_6

with animals is a mystery, and it is a mystery we want to be free of. We do, but not all of us do. Many of the general public do not only want to continue to live with animals, they also want to live with animals in a different world, a world that is more just, where there is more solidarity and which is more human: the term "human" in fact integrates our animal side.

Imagining, however, that things could change without appearing naive is difficult on account of the inflexibility of social relations, and the destructive force of the economic policies that are widely in place throughout the world. How can we think of abandoning utilitarian relations with animals, given industrial capitalism and a globalized financial system where the human being is no more than an object in the economy in the service of the *classes possédantes*.[1] I know that this term is considered to be obsolete, or at the very least as having overtones, but it describes things as they are. There are those who have possessions, and others, humans, animals and non-humans, who are possessed. To be convinced of this, it is enough to work in the livestock industry, in production, abattoir or processing, where man and beast are treated in a similar way, as if they were material. As one abattoir worker explained: "More importance is given to animals than to human beings, because anyway, the animal has to be well-treated or it will have an effect on the meat, but human beings, who cares?... the price of a kilo of pork or other meat is more important than the price of a kilo of worker." It is enough to talk to the workers or the middle management of factories that are closing down, or listen to workers or public service managers who are being made redundant. The human being is no more than their short-term usefulness (or uselessness). The subjective person is denied, and this is why resistance to closures has used the subjective body: the face, or the naked body. It was by posing naked that the Chaffoteaux workers reminded us that they existed. It is by showing their faces that the Nokia workers reminded us that they were not objects (Porcher 2009). Human life has a price today, no longer implicit, and discretely left out of ethical discourse, but a fixed price, one where the state consents to save a sick person or care for the aged on a fixed budget, and this price tends to drop. How can we imagine giving a value to animal life when our life as human beings is denied and we are becoming merchandise, as marketable body parts have a higher value on the stock exchange than our working bodies? We are becoming beasts ourselves in a butcher's that has no faith

[1] Translator's note: the moneyed classes, literally the classes who possess.

or law, in the image of the livestock industry: animal matter, human matter, sold to the highest bidder.

It is therefore difficult to be optimistic for ourselves and for animals. But we can dream, for millions of people dream of a different world—and perhaps the animals themselves dream with us. So let us imagine what domestic animals dream: of what world, of what relations with humans? How can we plan this utopia where animals will have a good life with us?

Imagine a world shaped by the "politics of civilization" proposed by Edgar Morin (2008), a world built on intelligence and generosity instead of stupidity and greed, a world which prioritizes quality of life, or rather, in my view, life itself: a life lived, a sentient life, a life connected to everything that lives. As Caillé pointed out, past socialist utopias no longer seem credible (Caillé et al. 2011), despite, in my opinion, their driving force living on, the hope that they still bring, and what we have been bequeathed by those who fought before us for a life worth living. These utopias, however, do not integrate the constraints that we can no longer deny, caused by the fact that we live in a finite world in which we cannot produce more and consume more indefinitely. To my mind, the convivial society that we are invited to build by Caillé following Ivan Illich allows us to re-give a grandeur to, and go further than the revolutionary utopias in order to enable them to exist, because it is still relevant to be "communist": to share, not to strain after property and accumulation; to be "socialist": to think together, with solidarity; to be "anarchist": to think for ourselves and to refuse to bend the knee.

Imagine then, that we could have a revolution, that is to say that we could effectively change the foundations of society, that we could break with our wretched and unthinking relations with life and with our alienated relations at work, that we could finally be genuinely sensuous. Imagine, as Alain Caillé wrote, that we could find "a way of living together, democratically, and with dignity, without massacring each other" (2011). It would mean producing freely and sharing wealth, and therefore accepting being less wealthy so that others can be more so. What is more necessary for being happy than everybody around you being happy too?

Imagine that this convivial society can be a reality, not just tomorrow, but for "future generations". In the meantime, however, what form would this utopia of living with animals, for animals and for ourselves, take? It should be understood that this would not involve defending "traditional" farming; rather, it would involve inventing another life at work, which has learned the lessons of the past and seizes the potential in the present, and the benefits of a science "of proximity" which brings together imagination, listening, rigueur and a duty to the public good.

The question of work, not just as a concept closely tied to industrial capitalism, but as a living relationship with the world, is central for domestic animals, as it is for ourselves. We must transform work in order for animals to live on good terms with us. This requires rethinking wild/domestic relations, the status of animals at work, the nature of work with animals and its sense as well as their place in work and the conditions of life at work, for them, and for us.

Wild and Domestic: The Wolf and the Sheep

As we have seen above, issues surrounding animal husbandry do not only concern farm animals, but they also concern all domestic animals, and reflect on so-called "wild" animals. We can observe a dissolution in our engagement with domestic animals in favour of animals that are now only "wild" in name. An example of this can be observed in the changes in our representations of sheep and wolves.

Social relations with animals built on domestication have become banal in collective representations and are very often seen as "natural", for who is surprised to see a cow in a meadow and sheep in the mountains or to live with a dog? It needs to be stressed, however, in what way this life with animals is "above-natural" and surprising. As we have seen, social relations of production engage human beings and animals, and human societies and animal societies, and have done so since the dawn of the process of domestication. If, as Caillé wrote (2007b) after Mauss, "the tie means more than the commodity" in human societies, or as he explains of the gift relation, "the value of the tie is of more importance than the value of the usage and the value of the exchange", the same is true when we consider society as not only an association of humans but also as an association of humans and animals. As we have seen with farmers of animals, relations between humans and animals involve more than the economic interests of humans. We do not do animal husbandry to make money off the backs of animals, but because we want to live with them, and the best way to do that is by procuring an income from them which will permit us to have both an economic life and a shared life with animals. How, for example, can an elephant driver feed his elephant if it has lost its work to mechanization?

As the authors of "*Tombeau de l'éléphant d'Asie*"[2] have shown, this very engaging domestic animal is on the point of disappearing because of the transformations in its environment and in agricultural work, without its cultural and affective importance and the importance of its company having been taken into account (Bisque and Javron 2002).[3]

This is why farmers, and all of us with them, have a debt to farm animals, and their protection is one of the minimum terms of the exchange. In the conflicts between sheep farmers and pro-wolf activists, farmers cannot leave "the wolf his share" as ecologists demand, because they have a duty of protection towards their animals which absolutely prohibits abandoning them to predators. It would be a profound denial of the sense of their profession. Nor is it enough to reimburse farmers as they breed their animals for the abattoir anyway; that would be a misunderstanding. As we have seen, the mortal fate of animals categorically excludes neither the duty of protection, nor the attachment that farmers can have for their sheep.

Note that today, the changes in representations of what domestic or "wild" animals are go hand in hand with a palpable enlargement of the notion of "domestic animal". For because as humans we occupy nearly the whole earth, there is a tendency now to offer our protection to these animals that up until now have been excluded from our relations. We offer our protection to all those who we consider stakeholders in our earthly domus, to those who are important to us, and therefore matter to us. Wolves, bears, crows and whales share our home, to varying degrees depending on our culture. They are no longer "wild". This change in the status of animals in our societies, and the labile character of "wild" animals, is apparent in our multiple relations with them. In our societies, wild/domestic representations have been inverted to a great degree. "Wild" animals are no longer red in tooth and claw, cruel and without law, but have become free, socialized and intelligent, unlike domestic animals, who are no longer gentle and peaceful beings, but either individuals who we tend to give an identity to, sometimes even giving them their own identity papers, as is the case with dogs, or, like pigs or chickens, they are imbecilic things that we can exploit like raw material. Wild animals are no longer foils, they are models. Starting from the position that this is why

[2] Translator's note: "The Fall of the Asian Elephant".

[3] On the subject of work relations with elephants, see also the delightful film "*Sunny et l'éléphant*" by Frédric Lepage. Studio Canal, 2008.

the legitimate place for animals on earth must now be negotiated between animals—or their spokespeople[4]—and us, a different category from the wild/domestic opposition seems pertinent to represent "non-humans", as Latour proposed in a more general context. This category should cover animals with whom we want to live, as opposed to animals with whom we do not want to live: not theoretically, but really live with, in the same place. If we want to live with wolves and bears, if we want to give them a place in a world which our ancestors, not without reason, excluded them from, if we accommodate them in the mountains where sheep can be found, they change status. I have two comments however: our ancestors banished wolves and bears because they devoured their sheep. Considering that it is still a sheep farmer's duty to protect their animals, and that neither wolves nor bears have changed, they have not become herbivores, this change poses a problem. As prophesied by Isiah, We suddenly want the wolf to lie down with the lamb. Reality, however, resists this, and short of equipping them with a rumen and turning them into ruminants, it is necessary to separate them in order to protect one and allow the other to live.

At all events, and providing for any necessary political action, it seems essential that we remember what having domesticated animals means: what it meant for our ancestors and what it means to us. It would certainly be convenient if there were no choice to make, if the wolf and the lamb could lie down together, as it is written, but in the meantime, more mundanely, the debt that we owe to farm animals imposes on us the need to make a choice. First respect the farmers and protect the sheep, offer them peaceful living conditions by not living in fear of wolves, and then find a place for wolves, if it is possible. The paradox of this situation is surely by *voluntarily* making a place for wolves, we are making it a domestic animal. But will the wolves agree?

The opposition between wild and domestic, as Micoud pointed out (2010), is neither biological nor ecological but anthropological, and this allows the author to propose a new double opposition, first between animals that are "naturalized living wild" and pastoral or ecological animals, and second between the living-being (pets) and the living-material (animals for production). It should be noted, however, that even so-called

[4] For farmers, however, animals are not "dumb entities", they are "non-humans" who act and prompt action, not like a scallop or a lake, but because as our attachments are not imaginary, and rest on an inter-subjective relationship, we act with them precisely because they are not dumb.

living-material are living-being for workers. The living-material only exists in work procedures and organization, and this is precisely why the massive slaughter of animals is an immense source of suffering.

The Status of Domestic Animals

I would like to propose another way of considering the place of animals, from the perspective of our relations, particularly our relations with work. The wild/domestic opposition comes down to this opposition: animals with whom we can live and work and who want to live and work with us, and animals who we prefer not to live with, and who prefer not to live with us.

Domestic animals are characterized by their place in the social world, and particularly in the productive world. I believe that domestic animals can be defined as species, but also as individuals, on different levels: the first level would be insertion into production, the second level, insertion into work, and the third level, the nature of work. These levels would refer to the de facto cognitive and relational competences of animals and their status in work.

The first level would concern animals used on production processes where there is no need of an intentional reciprocal relationship between humans and these animals. This would include, for example, until proved to the contrary, insects, snails, crustaceans, frogs and fish.

The second level would concern animals engaged, not in production, but in work. That is to say in a production where the results also depend indirectly (rabbits, poultry, laboratory mice), or directly (cattle, sheep, zebus, pigs), on the relations animals have with humans and the quality of those relations, or even on the implication of those animals in work.

The third level would allow for the contextualization of work. What field of work are animals implicated in? I would suggest distinguishing in this way, depending on the country under consideration, because this area can evidently vary: pastoral domestic animals (cows, sheep, pigs, reindeer, zebus, camels), service domestic animals (dogs—and dogs have many different jobs which should be studied as such—horses, zoo and circus animals) and urban domestic animals (dogs, cats, parrots).

There are many questions to answer regarding pastoral domestic animals. Does an animal participate in production work which rapidly and directly takes their life, such as hogs, lambs, or calves, or indirectly participate, as is the case with sows, cows and buffalo cows, or is the animal not necessarily engaged, as with horses? What do they contribute to production? What do they produce? Do they "work"? The answer to this last question necessitates defining the concept of a "working" animal, as we will see later.

This proposition has several points of interest. On the one hand, it allows us to put to one side the notion of "livestock" animals, which is still very often used as synonymous with farm animals, and which seems inappropriate to work relations with animals today. This proposition, on the other hand, allows us to describe domestic animals, not in terms of their species, but in terms of work relations with them; for instance, dogs in China or cows in India are not the same domestic animals as they are in France. Furthermore, this proposition encourages a consideration of the status of those animals known as "wild" who are implicated in work, for example, primates at a zoo or wolves at an animal park, as well as what we expect from them through their insertion in work. Considering, as we have seen, that the relational rationality comes first for farmers, in other words, that it is more important than the economic rationality (Porcher 2002a, b), could we not think of farming as more than being constructed from the uses it furnishes us with? Must we not think about that we eat every day, *and* the competences of those animals in work as well? What is the difference between dogs and pigs? Not a great deal in terms of their competences at work. What are pigs capable of doing?

We should remember that farm animals are constructed by production and by work. An animal that no longer has a place in work faces extinction. It is important therefore to know what we can do together if we want to live with these animals.

A Good Job

Doing a good job is a central demand in the working world (Dejours 1993) because this good job is a path to recognition and to pleasure. Farmers also aspire to doing a good job with their animals, and, as I have proposed above, it is credible that the animals themselves also prefer good work relations to bad ones, being happy to being miserable, being loved to being mistreated.

The question of animals at work raises three important sub-questions: first, concerning the living conditions at work, second, the place of death for animals in work, and third, the place of animals in work.

Our living conditions and the living conditions of farm animals are tied to the organization of work. Suppose, in the framework of our utopia, that considering the negative record of the industrial century, we entered into a process of de-industrialization, that we made a clear break with industrial farming and procedures. Suppose we finished with the process of concentration and intensification, finished with the race for performance, finished with violence and suffering and finished with our submission to the dictates of the sector. Members of the public, farmers and animals, we would finally be free to participate in the convivial society to which many of us aspire, a society where the tie would take precedence over merchandise, a society where everyone, including animals, would have a place.

Living Conditions at Work

If agriculture ceased to be an industrial activity in the hands of a sector that is obsessed with short-term profit and competes against itself accordingly, here would no longer be 300,000 "professional" farms in France, nor the 100,000 that are competitive and performing in on the global market towards which we are progressing,[5] but there would be a million or more other farms. France could secure thousands of small or medium-sized farms for itself, managed individually or collectively with the support of generous state subsidies for agriculture, for agriculture is the primary public service and food independence is an indispensable condition for a nation's independence. It would not be a question of producing more, more quickly and more cheaply in the service of agri-food and agri-chemical shareholders: in a well-considered decrease, the question would be to produce in a way that accords with our shared need. We know that malnutrition is not actually the result of under-production, but of speculation and an unequal redistribution of food resources. Well-informed people of good will know that we can feed the nine billion inhabitants expected on our planet in 2050 without difficulty, if we produce and consume equitably and ecologically.

[5] This corresponds with scenario one, "agri-efficiency", in the forward-looking reflection "Agriculture, environment and territories, four scenarios for 2025; an exercise in forward perspective" by the *Groupe de La Bussière* French documentation 2006.

In France, the sale of produce from thousands of farms is done directly through local food systems, markets, the AMAP[6] and the Internet, (Chiffoleau et al. 2008; Lamine and Bellon 2010) or via "clusters", or the re-grouping of small and medium-sized enterprises with a common objective, based on the model of the cooperative fruit-growers in the region of Franche Compte, for example. Local food systems usually necessitate a farmer's implication in processing and selling their products, although some have neither the desire nor the skills to do so. I have, incidentally, heard many farmers expressing reservations about local food systems, which maintain domination ties between farmers and consumers whatever the intention, within the AMAP for example. It is indispensable that farmers be masters of their products. This does not invalidate associations or negotiations but it is important for farmers to not feel that they have exchanged one master for another. Unlike the vertical production chains put in place by modernizers and industrialists after the war which dispossessed farmers from their products, work and remuneration should be shared in an equitable manner.

In this farming on a human and animal scale, the size of herds is limited and mixed crop farming as well as mixed species animal husbandry is favoured. Grazing with the freedom to wander is required for all animals. Industrial breeds have been abandoned in favour of traditional breeds. The increase in production cycles has been taken into account, so the price of production, and therefore the sale price, is higher, but consumers learn to eat less and better, and some appreciate eating more and better. In our utopia, men would not be considered as waste more than animals would be. No one would ever again be driven to eat cheap food straight from the tin on a subway bench, before passing a short night on a flea-bitten duvet provided by a charity.

Animal farming systems would be designed to allow animals to have a good life, as far as the animal condition, and the human condition, permits. Animal happiness comes from simple things such as freedom, ties, care and respect. Freedom does not mean leaving them to their own devices and it is important that animals have at their disposal a habitat that "fits" them; one that does not just fit them physically, but fits in with their world. What does "*inhabit*" mean to a farm animal? The question is far from simple,

[6] *Association pour le maintain d'un agriculture paysanne* (Association for the maintenance of family farming).

and, to my knowledge, it has never been asked in this way before. This is why it is important for our utopia. What is a good home for a pig or pigs?

We could think more generally that we could negotiate a way of working with animals collectively, and we could take into account the animals' point of view and that of farmers of animals, consumers, and more broadly, of the general public. The question of working hours is therefore central, for both human beings and animals.

The way that time is thought of in work relations can completely transform work. Thinking of work in time units is not the same thing as thinking in a "task-oriented" way. This is what the historian of the working classes, E. P. Thompson, pointed out (2004) when he wrote that the appearance of clocks and watches in houses, schools and manufacturers radically transformed work and greatly contributed to its degradation through the measurement of work hours, controls, time keepers, sanctions and productivity research, or product quantity/time quantity. Time has become money. This insertion of time into work with animals was done by the pioneers of zootechnics, and optimized by their successors. There is an issue with "saving time", and "reducing unproductive time" throughout the scientific organization of agricultural work. As Lacombe wrote in 1952: in dairy production, "the machine can easily reduce milking time by more than half when it is correctly adjusted. The consequence is, however, that it is necessary to time yourself and to pay attention to every action, to avoid doing anything useless". Petting animals, talking to them, grooming them so that they are clean and pleasing to the eye, count as "useless actions".

We must first change our relations with time, in order to change the lives of animals as well as our own, because one makes no sense without the other, and therefore thinking about a future for animals outside of our own future is impossible. What would count then, would not be the time that a task such as milking cows and taking pigs out to pasture takes, it would be the quality of the time taken and the quality of the results produced. Taking animals to the meadow or along mountain paths is a pleasure that farmers well know, and know that their animals share. It is a relationship with animals, with nature and with self, that is not measureable.

Viewing work in a task-oriented way also reduces what psychologically is an artificial separation of work and private life, although from the point of view of the organization of work, this separation is considered real. The fact that this split has no validity is stressed by Fiorelli (2010) in relation to multi-activity farmers of animals, for whom work relations are exactly oriented towards the task, unlike other jobs, such as in the post office, where it is counted in units of time. This is why some farmers say that they are taking a break when doing animal husbandry. To outsiders, this supplementary work can appear, on the contrary, exhausting. What allows task-oriented work is a job that fits our human and animal potential. We can, as Marx wrote (1846/1982, p. 1065), "do something today, something else tomorrow, hunting in the morning, fishing in the afternoon, animal husbandry in the evening and engage in criticism after dinner, according to our desire, without ever becoming a hunter, fisherman, shepherd or critic".

Considering task-oriented work in this way would also change the lives of animals, because for animals in the livestock industry, as we have seen, there is nothing outside of work. A sow is in the factory 24 hours a day, and unlike workers, for whom the ringing of a bell finishes work, for a sow, a battery-farmed chicken or a cow on zero grazing, there is no end to work.

Another component of a good job which relates to the question of time is the form well-done work takes, and the values to which it is tied. As Crawford remarked in an appeal for manual and artisanal work (2010), the quest for well done work goes hand in hand with a practical generosity and with values such as solidarity and respect. An example of this would be taking *x* hours to repair a motorbike and then billing much lower, because your objective was to find the fault for the pure pleasure of going deeper and overcoming resistance, and not to bill your client for the maximum hours, like the most vulgar New York lawyer in a Grisham novel. Solidarity, which was a peasant value for a long time, and which has been replaced today by vicious competition, is a component of a good job. Crawford also pointed out the place of experience in knowledge. To quote a doubtless apocryphal saying attributed to Einstein, "only experience is knowledge, the rest is information". Between information and experience, there is the implication of the body in work, there are successes and failures, suffering and pleasure.

The Place of Animal Death in Work

Must we continue to conceal animal slaughter, and thus reassure consumers through removing the need to think? For me, the answer is no. The death of farm animals is, like the conditions of their lives, our collective responsibility. It seems to me that by giving visibility to abattoirs, we could progress towards the emergence of collective debate that could participate in a real transformation of this activity. For the fate of a farm animal is the abattoir, but at what moment? For what animals? To fulfil what necessity? In what way?

The painful crux of our relations with domestic animals, including dogs, cats and parrots, is death: the visible death of farm animals, or the hidden death cats or dogs in pet shops or animal refuges. In our utopia, hidden death would no longer exist. If time were no longer money, but a tie, there would be no rush.

How should the death of farm animals, of cows and pigs, be? Must we follow the path proposed by animal rights activists? It is because the consequences of "animal liberation" would be worse than the wrong they claim to denounce that I think that this is a false path. Eating living death is much worse, from an anthropological point of view, than killing animals and thus circulating life between us and them. Liberating animals in order to remove their death would lead to a rupture with them, and in our utopia, the objective, on the contrary, would be to live with animals, and re-enforce our attachments. Nevertheless, the question of the death of animals, for animals, remains. For animals do not want to die and we know that. The question remains, particularly because of the changing sensibility of farmers with regard to animals. As we have seen, there are now vegetarian farmers. There are also farmers who would really be content with only 20 cows, even with 2 or 3.

Why do we kill animals? One reason, historically, is nutritional. However, before the expansion of "the meat industry", the consumption of meat was limited, even if it was qualitatively important. Another reason is that pragmatically, a farmer cannot keep all his animals any more than the owner of a cat can keep all the kittens that the cat gives birth to. As we have seen, farmers must make an income from the presence of their animals so that they can live with them. Animal reproduction and the sale of the young are a means of making relations durable.

In this utopian animal husbandry, the object would therefore not be to make the death of animals disappear. But we can imagine other rules governing the retirement of animals, or of slaughter. First of all, this should concern the choice of breeds, as they determine the life expectancy of animals. Rather than slaughtering industrial pigs at five and a half months, it would be better to breed Limousin pigs up to the age of 18 months. What difference does it make, you may ask? It makes a difference to the pigs;

but the question is what work a pig can do with us. Is providing us with meat all that it can do? In my opinion, it is not. Pigs can have many other jobs, particularly in the forest, but we should interest ourselves in their competences at the heart of an agrarian system. It is the same for calves and lambs. If the gift and counter gift between animals and us is expressed by a good life for the animals, they must have more time to live their lives.

If, for example, as I will return to in the following section, animals have an active place in work, the question of when to retire them must be asked. Many farmers, particularly of goats, do not send their old animals to the abattoir, but construct a sub-herd, retired from production but not from the collective. This is why animal life expectancy is an important element the debate.

The question is equally important concerning dairy production. For a cow to have milk, it must have a calf. This calf, which you could say is "for the butcher", is fed on artificial milk for three months and is then sent to the abattoir. Why not leave the calf with its mother and only take half of the cow's milk, as was done in the past before zootechnics specialized animals and separated "dairy" cows from "lactating" cows, or those who feed a calf? A return from the specialization of species, a process that began at the beginning of the nineteenth century, is not impossible, even if it must inevitably go hand in hand with a drastic reduction in the amount produced and consumed. It may seem very difficult to certain farmers for whom work is at base productivist, as I have heard expressed, to content themselves with the 4000 or 5000 litres of milk that one cow can produce alone because it does not require a big technical effort on the part of farmers. What would be the point? This view ignores the fact that asking a cow to pour forth more than 10,000 litres of milk is not actually addressing the limits of the work it is capable of doing.

Thus, we can see that we need to rethink farm work with animals by considering their interests. The desire of many farmers is not to remove death, but to postpone it for as long as possible, and this desire is shared by many members of the general public.

This, however, still leaves the question of a good death. Is a "good" abattoir possible? I think it is. A "good" abattoir would not hide itself, would permit the farmer to accompany the animals or not, depending on their feelings. It would allow those who work with the carcass to do a good job, an A-to-Z job, the job of a craftsman.

The proposal for a mobile abattoir which I and the designer Eric Daru put forward provoked much discussion, and I received an enormous amount of mail after the publication of an article on the subject (Porcher and Daru 2005). The large majority of farmers want something else for their animals other than an industrial abattoir, and we should rethink the process of slaughter with them, but also with the general public. The slaughter of animals must not be taken on by workers bearing alone responsibility for the death of animals. Farm animals have a common tie, and when that tie is undone, we must all bear the responsibility for their death.

The slaughter of animals, as it has been done, is not the model to follow, and I think it is possible to open new avenues. As M. Joel Jernez, an old vet,[7] testified, there were ways of doing it not so long ago that bore witness to the respect that we can have for animals, and the base from which we can work anew:

> There was still a municipal abattoir and I remember the slaughter of a bullock in 1983, which preserved sense and relations with animals. The butcher was local, and was the last breeder of this Charolais Normand ("yellow") cross breed, which weighed one thousand kilograms, and had been put out to pasture at the end of his working life. I saw him come down from his van and lead the bullock to the slaughter room, which must have been fifty meters square. The bullock followed in a docile manner, proving that it was used to being led, and it showed no sign of nervousness. The butcher took his mallet from the pocket of his black smock and turned to face the bullock. He said "Ok, old boy, it's your turn", and he knocked it out. The bullock collapsed with a little whimper and a few convulsions when the butcher passed a wire through the hole made by the mallet, and down the spinal cord. The butcher waited a good five minutes, which was, he explained, a tradition, and this I found inexplicable.[8] Then he washed his hands and put on a clean white shirt. He slit its throat well below the cervical aorta at the base of the neck, and after this he skinned it, gutted it and split the carcass in half. I think, rightly or wrongly, that if the bullock felt pain, it did not suffer, at least much less than it would have done in the production line slaughter generally found today. The fact that he had talked to the bullock is very significant, even if the words were perhaps more ritualistic than personal.

[7] I am reporting what the vet told me personally.

[8] This is also what the slaughter man who came to kill my lambs did. The reason was that he wanted to be sure that the animal was really dead before any intervention. He verified its death afterwards by the lack of eye movement.

Talking to animals is a way of taking responsibility for our actions. As we can see in this evocation, doing the whole job also changes the sense of work, and this would mean, in a "good" abattoir, renouncing the taylorization of work and taking time to reflect on what you are doing and why, not only concerning the content of work, but also its visibility. To my mind, it is necessary to make animal death visible once more, to no longer do something shameful. This means also rethinking the architecture of an abattoir, and its insertion into the urban or rural landscape.

The Collaboration of Animals in Work

Contrary to mainstream theories, I propose that rather than "liberating animals" from work and therefore signalling the "end of work" with them, it would be better for them and for us to make work emancipating. To do this, it is necessary to understand what place animals have in work. Starting with the hypothesis, based on my experience of working in animal husbandry, that animals are not purely work objects but they are equally actors, it is necessary to demonstrate their participation in work, that is, their collaboration, even their cooperation. For example, cows collaborate with the work of milking on a farm equipped with a robotic milking system. They put their affective and cognitive capacities to work to do so (Porcher and Schmitt 2010). Pigs do the job that the farmer expects of them but they do much more, or differently, just as the wild boars or vultures do in an animal park (Chartier and Porcher 2009). Most farmers sense this collaboration with animals in work, even though they find it difficult to think of in these terms, as historically, the word "work" in the context of animals has been applied to draught animals.

We should therefore emphasize this "animal working", that is to say, we should describe and understand what we mean by "working" when applied to an animal, whether they be domestic or not (for example, circus animals), and we should then draw conclusions about the organization of work (Porcher 2011).

While I was a farmer of animals, I was often surprised by the implicit collective nature of the work that shaped me, my ewes and my dog. On an ordinary day, after the alarm clock tore me from my bed, I joined the ewes to milk them, still half asleep. Before the sheep dog arrived, I watched their movements and listened to them bleating, and to the sounds that told me that the night was over, even in winter when it was still dark. I pushed open the door, and I saw the ewes lying down amidst the fragrance of the straw, one next to another, or alone and isolated. Some of them stretched themselves, and got up with slow movements, as they watched me install the milking equipment. They stood up gradually because of my approach, and organized themselves. The oldest one took her place on the milking platform, well in advance of the timing. Another took her place in the queue behind her, as if she had important things to do coming up and wanted to get through the constraints of work as quickly as possible. I only interfered with the order in which they passed if there were disagreements between them, and bad-tempered locking of horns. I knew that I could only milk them with their consent; their organized participation and these ties with work, between amity and authority, amazed me. After I had worked in the cheese dairy, we went back to the mobile sheep pen where I had put them the day before, and where the ewes passed the day. The dog had been on his toes since the alarm clock had rung, and without doubt, even before, and gave himself up totally to his job as sheep dog on the path. Each to his task, he went to the left and the right, trying to make an orderly and manageable line of the animals entrusted to his care. He directed a fixed glare at one young ewe, who responded by finding her place in the line without further comment. The dog knew what he had to do too, and I had nothing to add. It was better if I said nothing, as I had observed that I was more likely to slow things down by my incongruous orders, than offer effective advice. I watched him work, and his contentment in doing what he did amazed me and inspired my admiration. I had the feeling a thousand times during these daily return journeys that the animals understood the contentment of work that they knew they shared with us. Each attentive movement of the dog, each bound of the ewes mocking their guide, expressed the beauty of the world and *joie de vivre.* I felt it like a current passing from them to me, and from me to them, and I too found that everything was beautiful and deserved to be seen and shared. Work was the place of our unexpected meeting, and the occasion for our communication, even though we came from three different species that have been believed since the Neolithic, even the Neanderthal age, to have nothing to say to, and nothing to do with each other.

When I shared my surprise at this collaboration, the responses that I got all referred back to conditioning, genetic selection and innate competences, all responses that exclude animal intelligence and their cognitive and affective interest in participating in work. However, the hundreds of encounters that I have had with farmers and their animals in the course of my research demonstrate that farmers rely on their animals to work, but animals rely on their farmers to do what they have to do just as much. Moreover, it is the tie with work which engages both man and beast in gift relations and the tie judgements that I have described above.

As I have personally observed, one of the most important consequences of animals being recognized as actors in work is that their needs are not only "natural", but also relate to the world of work, although this does still need to be proved, notwithstanding the fact that results I have already obtained tend very clearly in that direction. One of the most underestimated needs is that of recognition. Although this need is recognized for a dog, whether it be a sheep dog, a guide dog or a rescue dog, it is completely overlooked for cows, sheep and pigs.

Although the consequences of these changes do not seem have been recognized as they should have been, the status of a dog at work has changed a lot. Hence in Norway in 2008, a judgement from the Supreme Court conferred the status of public servant on police dogs, meaning that all aggression directed against one would be considered in the same light as if it had been directed against the police themselves. Even though their status has not been so elevated in France, in 2009 the police dog Rin Tin Tin received a bronze medal for bravery and devotion in Paris.

The growing place of animals in work does not only concern dogs; in Germany, the police trained the vulture "Sherlock" to find missing persons (2010), although this should not be so surprising as vultures already work in animal parks; they take part in presentations in partnership with a falconer in public demonstrations of birds of prey. Like other working animals (dogs, as well as cows, sheep and pigs), they can respect the rules of work or not, be lazy or very active, and be a good partner or not. Work relations between vultures and falconers are based on confidence and negotiation, as they are with farmers.

Further, in human service jobs, either in hospitals or in private households, dogs have a growing place which is not however, considered as work but as mediation; the animal is not thought to be an actor in work, rather, merely a mediator between the human carer and the human in need of care. This approach, which comes from the behaviourist viewpoint of the theory of conditioning, makes it possible to bypass deeper reflection on the real place of animals at work. What do animals really do in relations with invalids and the disabled? What do they invent? We do not know and it seems to me that we prefer to think that they invent nothing, that it is us who give them commands. I believe that the animal is not a mediator but a carer in a relationship with the sick or disabled, and should be considered as such.

What do all these results and anecdotes lead us to, when considering the organization of work?

Unlike the academic study of "animal welfare" with its obsession with figures and productivity, taking the collaboration of animals in work into account leads to a decentralization of the question of their welfare. As I have pointed out, it is not only a question of "welfare", but also of recognition. If animals bring something specific to work, either as an individual or collectively, that something must be recognized. However, upstream, it also means offering animals living conditions at work that are more in accord with their own world and with their competences and tastes.

It therefore involves putting some sort of "labour law" in place for domestic animals as a starting point, which would form the basis of our duties to animals depending on the work that we expect from them, and on what they expect from the work. We could imagine that in our utopia the gift of a good life for animals would be a prerequisite. A good life, as we have seen, means a life that is in accord with the animal world and its relational, cognitive and affective potentialities. It also means a habitat that is co-constructed with animals, a place where they can go or not go, and an individual or a collective space. It means diversified food that not only accords with the needs of animals, but equally with their tastes. It means an organization of work which respects the animals' rhythms, which takes into account relations animals have between themselves: the ties of friendship, the ties between mothers and their young but also ties of conflict. It means an organization of work which, as we have seen above, gives animals a chance to live their lives, and allows them a life expectancy that is congruent with this project, both inside and outside the field of production, so that for domestic animals, there is a life outside of work, and after the working years.

We can judge how utopian this project is by recalling that the majority of humans in this world of ours have no access to any of this. But if, as the United Nations Development Program has stressed, it is individuals that form the wealth of nations, making animals number amongst these individuals would without doubt offer a better chance to humans.

It is worth noting that this is the reason why the question of animal work is more relevant to the human sciences than to "natural science". Domestic animals relate to the human world of work and it is by considering work, that is to say, by studying society and the social and work relations we have with animals, that we can reach a better understanding of their place in work and in society. To understand ties between humans and animals in the social field is primarily to consider work, for it is work which draws us together and which sustains the tie between us. Without work, however discrete it may be, as with the work of pets, there are no ties.

Conclusion

At the end if this journey we have taken with farmers and their animals, I hope that I have left you, dear reader, more aware of the beauty and richness of animal husbandry. I hope that I have shared with you the love of animals that motivates real farmers, for far from my old questions as a neo-rustic plunged into the industrial inferno, I know now that animal husbandry has nothing to do with what those who have dominated subject for one hundred and fifty years have been saying. Animal husbandry is a tie that escapes them and therefore at heart, they know nothing, for they are lost in their pernicious habits. They are lost in the power they have to make money and they have limited their lives to this, and they want to limit our lives too. They believe they hold the meaning of history and they endlessly chase their own tails in pursuit of this certainty. They presume to talk about animal husbandry, and massacre millions of animals for economic reasons tied to public health. The horrified protests of the Maasai people over the mass graves of mad cow disease did not teach them anything. They have neither the sense of the gift nor of the debt. Figures outweigh life, and the folly of their ambitions in the face of the immense and fascinating potentialities of our relations with animals does not touch them at all. The world that they impose on us, these people who do not have "qualms", that they tell us is rational, realistic and pragmatic, is an imbecile world, vulgar and cruel. They do not know it yet, but their world belongs to the past. Contrary to what they pretend, modernity is not on their side, but on the side of those who are ready to question their cer-

J. Porcher, *The Ethics of Animal Labor*,
DOI 10.1007/978-3-319-49070-0

tainties, to re-invent their practices, to share their knowledge and ties that they have with animals and with nature.

How difficult it is to make others feel what it is to live and work with animals when it is not money but happiness that ties you to animals and to the world? How can these emotions, these fragrances, these tastes, this physical contact and these sounds be expressed? It is a whole universe of sensations experienced daily. How can you describe the way a ewe looks at her newborn lamb, and at you, who are there vigorously rubbing the lamb with a handful of straw so that it will not be cold and will want to suckle? How can you describe the scent of the fleece of a ewe that wafts behind the herd as they walk, and mixes with the misty morning air, a fragrance that is heady and sweet, that returns to me as I write and that I believe I can detect around me in my office now? How can you describe the sense of space that shepherds have as they traverse the mountains with their sheep: the solitude, the fear and the perfect happiness? What can we say about the ties with animals that have a thousand faces, a thousand forms and a thousand places?

Animal husbandry is found in each particular relation that a farmer maintains with his animals. It has a thousand faces but the faces all have one thing in common: the indispensable presence of animals. Whatever the differences in region and culture, all farmers are bound together and speak in a common language, that of ties with their animals and ties with nature. Meadows, forests, vales, marshes, mountain peaks and deserts all carry the imprint of animals, whether it be a ponderous footfall or a joyous gallop. All carry the imprint of our ties. We have had ten thousand years of life in common. And for ten thousand years, I imagine, domestic animals have been waiting for us to grow up and leave behind our brutal and redoubtable human infancy. How patient animals are! How compassionate! Do they pity us, as a worker in a pig farm once said to me?

We have seen that living with animals is not obvious. It is a utopia and it is a revolutionary utopia, for to continue to live with animals, we must change the world's foundations. In the world as it is, man will end up disappearing, being replaced by machines, becoming himself half-human, half-machine, a living death, eternal and empty, all-powerful in a world where nature is under his heel, but that is indifferent to his presence.

Before renouncing life, listen to the cattle grazing and the pigs sleeping. Listen to the animals speaking. Listen to them.

Bibliography

Alphandéry P., Sancébé Y, 2009. L'émergence de la sociologie rurale en France. Dans La sociologie rurale en questions. Etudes rurales n°183. Editions de l'EHESS, pp. 23–40

Alter N., 2009. Donner et prendre. La coopération en entreprise. Editions La Découverte/MAUSS

Alteroche d' F., 2004. Avec la méthode Optibrand , le tissu vasculaire rétinien donne l'empreinte digitale » des bovins. Réussir Bovins Viande. Novembre 2004

Arendt H., 1997. Eichmann à Jérusalem. Rapport sur la banalité du mal. Folio. Gallimard

Ariès P., 1975. Essai sur l'histoire de la mort en Occident, du Moyen Age à nos jours. Seuil

Bacqué M.F., 2003. Apprivoiser la mort. Editions Odile Jacob

Baratay E., Mayaud J.L. (dir.), 1997. L'animal domestique, XVIème-Xxème siècle. Cahiers d'histoire n°3–4, tome XLII, Lyon

Baratay E., 1996. L'église et l'animal. Editions du Cerf

Bauman Z., 2002. Modernité et holocauste, Paris, La Fabrique Editions

Bekoff M., 2009. Les émotions des animaux. Editions Payot

Bensaïd D., 2007. Les dépossédés. Karl Marx, les voleurs de bois et le droit des pauvres. La Fabrique Editions.

Bensoussan G., 1998. Auschwitz en héritage ? Du bon usage de la mémoire. Editions Mille et une nuits

J. Porcher, *The Ethics of Animal Labor*,
DOI 10.1007/978-3-319-49070-0

Bloch M., 1949. Apologie pour l'histoire ou métier d'historien. Cahiers des Annales 3. Librairie Armand Colin. En ligne sur le site: http://classiques.uqac.ca/classiques/bloch_marc/apologie_histoire/apologie_histoire.ht

Bodson L., 2001. Les animaux dans l'Antiquité: un gisement fécond pour l'histoire des connaissances naturalistes et des contextes culturels », dans/in Acta Orientalia Belgica, 14, 2001: L'animal dans les civilisations orientales. Henri LIMET in honorem, pp. 1–27.

Boltanski L., 2009. De la critique. Précis de sociologie de l'émancipation. Gallimard

Boltanski L., Chiappelo E., 1999. Le nouvel esprit du capitalisme. NRF. Gallimard

Bourdieu P., 1984. Questions de sociologie. Les Editions de minuit

Bourdieu P., 2003. Méditations pascaliennes. Points. Seuil

Boutang P.A., 2004. L'Abécédaire de Gilles Deleuze. Entretiens avec Claire Parnet. A comme Animal. Editions Montparnasse. En ligne sur de nombreux sites internet

Brisebarre A.M., 1998. La mort des animaux: un mal nécessaire? Etudes rurales 147–148, pp. 9–14

Busquet G, Javron J.M., 2002. Tombeau de l'éléphant d'Asie. Editions Chandeigne

Caillé, A., 1994. Don, intérêt et désintéressement. La Découverte

Caillé A., 2000 Anthropologie du don. Le tiers paradigme. Desclée de Brouwer

Caillé A. (dir.), 2007a. La quête de reconnaissance. Nouveau phénomène social total. La Découverte/MAUSS

Caillé A., 2007b. « Don et association », Revue du MAUSS permanente, 1er décembre 2007 [en ligne]. http://www.journaldumauss.net/spip.php? article202

Caillé A., 2009. Théorie anti-utilitariste de l'action. Fragments d'une sociologie générale. La Découverte/MAUSS

Caillé A., Lazzeri C. (dir.), 2009. La reconnaissance aujourd'hui. CNRS Editions

Caillé A., Humbert M., Latouche S., Viveret P., 2011. De la convivialité. Dialogues sur la société conviviale à venir. La Découverte

de Charnacé, G. 1868, Considérations générales sur l'espèce ovine, dans Emile Baudement, 1868, Les mérinos, Librairie d'éducation et d'agriculture. De Charles Delagrave et Cie, pp. 37–38

de Gasparin P., 1843–1848. Cours d'agriculture. Volume I. Librairie Agricole de la Maison Rustique

Chartier A., Porcher J., 2009. Influence des conditions d'élevage en plein air sur le comportement des truies gestantes. 41ème Journées de la Recherche Porcine

Chiffoleau Y., Aubrée P., Berger B., Bernard C., 2008. Les circuits courts: bien manger sur les territoires. Editions Educagri

Coetzee J.M., 2004. Elisabeth Costello. Seuil

Colson F., 1980. Modernization de la production porcine: les limites économiques au processus de rationalisation de l'élevage porcin. Journées de la Recherche Porcine 1980. pp. 59–71

Crawford M.B., 2010. Eloge du carburateur. Essai sur le sens et la valeur du travail. La Découverte

Damien M., Kastler A., Nouet J.C., 1981. Le grand massacre. Editions Fayard
Dantzer R.. Mormède P., 1979. Le stress en élevage intensif. Editions Masson/INRA
Davezies P., 1993. Mobilisation de la personnalité et santé au travail, dans Intervention au colloque « l'action des collectivités territoriales en matière de santé et de sécurité au travail ». Lyon, février 1993
Dedieu B., Sabourin E., (sous la direction de): Le travail en agriculture, son organization et ses valeurs face à l'innovation. Editions l'Harmattan
Dejours C., 1993. Travail, usure mentale. Bayard
Dejours C., 1998. Souffrance en France. La banalisation de l'injustice sociale. Seuil
Dejours C., 2003. L'évaluation du travail à l'épreuve du réel. Critique des fondements de l'évaluation. Editions Quae
Dejours C., 2009. Travail Vivant. Tome 1 Sexualité et travail, tome 2 Travail et émancipation. Payot
Descola P., 2005. Par delà nature et culture. Gallimard
Despret V., 2002. Quand le loup habitera avec l'agneau. Les Empêcheurs de penser en rond
Despret V., 2007. Bêtes et hommes. Catalogue de l'exposition "Bêtes et hommes". La Villette. 2007. Gallimard
Despret V., 2009. Penser comme un rat. Collection Sciences en questions. Editions Quae
Dewitte J., 1993. La donation première de l'apparence. De l'anti-utilitarisme dans le monde animal selon A. Portmann. Revue du Mauss n°1. Editions La Découverte
Dickens P., 1996. Reconstructing nature. Alienation, emancipation and the division of labour. Routledge
Digard J.P., 1990. L'homme et les animaux domestiques. Anthropologie d'une passion. Collection Le temps des sciences. Editions Fayard
Digard J.P., 2005. Les Français et leurs animaux. Hachette
Dodier N., 1995. Les hommes et les machines. Métailié
Dumont R., 1946. Le problème agricole français. Esquisse d'un plan d'orientation et d'équipement. Bibliothèque de l'économie contemporaine. Les éditions nouvelles
Fabre-Vassas C., 1994. La bête singulière. NRF. Editions Gallimard
Fairlie S., 2010. Meat: a benign extravagance. Hyden House Ltd
Ferret S., 2000. Les humains. Flammarion
Fiorelli C., 2010. L'aménagement des conditions de vie au travail des éleveurs. Proposition d'un cadre d'analyse des relations entre rapport subjectif et organization du travail en élevage. Etude de cas chez les éleveurs pluriactifs. Thèse d'AgroParisTech. Spécialité Zootechnie. Soutenue le 2 novembre 2010
Fiorelli C., Porcher J., Dedieu B., 2007. Pourquoi faire de l'élevage quand on a un autre travail ? Rencontres Recherches Ruminants, 14, pp. 389–392

Fleischer R., 1974. Soylent green. Swashbuckler Films, 1h37

Foer J.S., 2011. Faut-il manger les animaux ? Editions de l'Olivier

Fontenay E. de, 1998. Le silence des bêtes. Editions Fayard

Foucauld de J.B., 2009. « Gorz et le temps choisi, un débat inachevé », Revue du MAUSS permanente, 10 mars 2009 [en ligne]. http://www.journaldumauss.net/spip.php?article481

Francione Gary L., 2000. Introduction to Animal Rights. Your Child or the Dog, Temple University Press, Philadelphie

Gaignard, L., Charon, A., 2005. Gestion de crise et traumatisme : les effets collatéraux de la "vache folle". De l'angoisse singulière à l'embarras collectif. Travailler, 14, 57–71

Gautier A., 1990. La domestication. Et l'homme créa l'animal. Jardin des Hespérides. Editions Errance

Giraudon D., 2006. La nuit de Noël en Bretagne. Revue Armen, n°155, nov-déc. 2006. http://www.armen.net/2010/12/dossiers/ethnologie/la-nuit-de-noel-dans-la-civilisation-rurale/

Gorz A., 2008. Le travail dans la sortie du capitalisme. Revue ECOREV n°28 – En ligne. http://ecorev.org/spip.php?article641

Gould S.G., 1993. Comme les huit doigts de la main. Editions du Seuil

Gould S.J., 1997. L'éventail du vivant, le mythe du progrès. Editions du Seuil

Grandin T., 1997. Penser en images. Editions Odile Jacob

Haraway D., 2010. Manifeste des espèces de compagnie. Chiens, humains et autres partenaires. Terra cognita. Editions de l'Eclat

Haudricourt A.G., 1962. Domestication des animaux, culture des plantes et traitement d'autrui, dans La technologie science humaine, 1987. Editions Maison des Sciences de l'homme. pp. 37–46

Hemsworth P., Coleman G.J., 2010. Human-livestock interactions: the stockperson and the productivity and welfare of intensively farmed animals. CABI Publishing, 2nd edition

Henry M., 1987. La barbarie. PUF

Herman P., 2008. Les nouveaux esclaves du capitalisme : agriculture intensive et régression sociale. Editions Au Diable Vauvert

Hervieu B., Viard J., 2001. L'archipel paysan. La fin de la république agricole. Editions de l'Aube

Holm J., Jokka T., 2008. Filière animale et climat – l'influence négative de l'UE, Janvier 2008. Une publication de la délégation du parti de gauche suédois au GU NGL – http://www.meatclimate.org/home

Honneth A., 2000. La lutte pour la reconnaissance. Editions du Cerf

Ingold T. (dir.), 1988. What is an animal. Routledge. London

Jankélévitch V., 1977. La mort. Champs. Flammarion

Jankelévitch V., 1994. Penser la mort. Editions Liana Levi

Jussiau R., Montméas L., Parot J.C., 1999. L'élevage en France. 10 000 ans d'histoire. Educagri Editions

Kaprielian N., 2011. La mort par la viande. Les Inrockuptibles. 12 janvier 2011, pp. 31–37

Klemperer V., 1996. LTI, la langue du IIIème Reich. Agora. Pocket

Kropotkine P., 2002/1919. L'entraide. Editions Tops/H.Trinquier. Antony (92)

L'aménagement des conditions de vie au travail des éleveurs. Proposition d'un cadre d'analyse des relations entre rapport subjectif et organization du travail en élevage

Lacombe R., 1952. La traite mécanique. Collection La Terre. Flammarion

Lamine C., Bellon S., 2010. Transitions vers l'agriculture biologique. Pratiques et accompagnements pour des systèmes innovants. Editions Educagri

Landais E., Bonnemaire J., 1996. La zootechnie, art ou science ? Le Courrier de l'Environnement de l'Inra n°27, pp. 23–44

Larrere C., Larrere L., 1997. Le contrat domestique, dans le Courrier de l'Environnement de l'Inra n°30, pp 5–17

Larribe P., 2010. Du cadavre au défunt ou du placard au salon avant de quitter la scène. Etudes sur la mort, 2010, n°137, pp. 133–140

Latouche S., 2011. Les voies de la décroissance. Pour une société d'abondance frugale. In Caillé A., Humbert M., Latouche S., Viveret P., 2011. De la convivialité. Dialogues sur la société conviviale à venir. La Découverte

Latour B., 1999. Politiques de la nature. Comment faire entrer les sciences en démocratie. La Découverte

Latour B., 2006. Changer de société. Refaire de la sociologie. La Découverte

Latulipe H., 2001. Bacon. Documentaire. 82 mn Office National du Film du Canada

Levi P., 1987. Si c'est un homme. Pocket. Editions Julliard

Levi P., 1998. Conversations et entretiens. Bibliothèque 10/18. Editions Robert Laffont

Lévi-Strauss C., 2001. La leçon de sagesse des vaches folles, Études rurales, Jeux, conflits, représentations. http://etudesrurales.revues.org/document27.html

Lokhorst C., Groot Koerkamp P.W.G. (ed.), 2009. Precision livestock farming '09. Wageningen Academic Publishers

Malassis L., 1994. Nourrir les hommes. Flammarion

Malassis L., 2004. La longue marche des paysans. Fayard

Marx K., 1846/1982. L'idéologie allemande. Oeuvres philosophie. Bibliothèque de la Pléiade. Gallimard

Marx K., 1867/1994. Le Capital. 4Ème section. Oeuvres Economie I. Bibliothèque de la Pliéade. Gallimard

Mauss M., 1999/1923. Essai sur le don, dans Sociologie et anthropologie. Quadrige. Editions PUF, p. 258

Mayaud J.L., 2005. Gens de l'agriculture. La France rural 1940–2005. Chêne Editions

Mechin C., 1992. Bêtes à manger. Usages alimentaires des Français. Presses Universitaires de Nancy

Meda D., 1995. Le travail, une valeur en voie de disparition. Editions Aubier
Mendras H., 1984. La fin des paysans. Babel. Editions Actes Sud
Mepham B., 2006. The ethical matrix as a decision-making tool, with specific reference to animal sentience. In Turner J., D'Silva J. (eds.), Animals, ethics and trade: the challenge of animal sentience. Earthscan, London, UK, 134–145 n°30, pp. 5–17
Meuret M., 2010. Un savoir faire de bergers. Editions Quae/Educagri
Micoud A., 2010. Sauvage ou domestiques, des catégories obsolètes. Dans Sociétés. Relations anthropozoologiques. N°108. 2010/2, pp. 99–107
Midgley M., 1983. Animals and why they matter. The University of Georgia Press
Montméas L., Jussiau R., 1994. La zootechnie une discipline d'enseignement vue à travers les manuels scolaires: 1890/1970, dans Ethnozootechnie n°54
Moriceau J.M., 2005. Histoire et géographie de l'élevage français. Du moyen âge à la révolution. Fayard
Morin E., 2008. Pour une politique de civilisation. Editions Arléa
Morris W., 2010. Comment nous pourrions vivre. Présenté par Serge Latouche. Editions Le Clandestin
Mouret S., 2009. Le sens moral de la relation de travail entre hommes et animaux d'élevage : mises à mort des animaux et expériences morales subjectives d'éleveurs et de salariés. Thèse d'AgroParisTech. Soutenue en novembre 2009.
Mouret S., Porcher J., 2007. Les systèmes industriels porcins: la mort comme travail ordinaire. Natures, sciences, sociétés, 15, n°3, pp. 245–252
Noske B., 1989. Human and other animals. Beyond the boundaries of anthropology. London. Pluto
Ogor Y., 2009. Des éleveurs et de leur lutte contre l'humiliation. A propos du puçage électronique des animaux d'élevage. Dans Le travail mort-vivant. Notes et morceaux choisis n°8. Editions La Lenteur
Orwell G., 1949, 1984. Gallimard
Patou-Mathis M., 2006. Neanderthal, une autre humanité. Editions Perrin
Patterson C. 2008. Un éternel Treblinka. Calmann Levy
Pelletier N., Tyedmers P., 2010. Forecasting potential global environmental costs of livestock production 2000–2050 . PNAS Early edition. doi:10.1073/pnas.1004659107
Pereira C., 2009. Parler aux chevaux autrement. Une approche sémiotique de l'équitation. Dessins de Marine Oussedik. Photographies de Gérald Buthaud. Editions Amphora
Perez-Vitoria S., 2010. La riposte des paysans. Actes Sud
Phillips A., 2002. La mort qui fait aimer la vie. Darwin et Freud. Payot
Pilley J.W., Reid A.K., 2011. Border collie comprehends object names as verbal referents. Behavioral processes. In press
Porcher J., 2000. La mort n'est pas mon métier. Etudes sur la mort n°118. Editions L'esprit du Temps, pp. 29–48

Porcher J., 2002a. Eleveurs et animaux : réinventer le lien. Collection Partage du Savoir. Presses Universitaires de France. Prix Le Monde de la recherche universitaire 2002

Porcher J., 2002b. L'esprit du don, archaïsme ou modernité de l'élevage : éléments pour une réflexion sur la place des animaux d'élevage dans le lien social. Revue du Mauss n°20, Quelle autre mondialisation ? Editions La Découverte/ MAUSS, pp. 245–262

Porcher J., 2003. La mort n'est pas notre métier, Editions de l'Aube

Porcher J., Cousson-Gélie F., Dantzer R., 2004. Affective components of the human-animal relationship in animal husbandry. Development and validation of a questionnaire. Psychological Reports, 95, pp. 275–290

Porcher J., 2005. Le « bien-être animal » existe-t-il ? Economie rurale n°285, pp. 88–94

Porcher J., Daru E., 2005. Concevoir des alternatives à l'organization industrielle du travail. Un camion pour le transport et l'abattage des animaux. FaçSADe (INRA-SAD), n°2005-23; repris dans Campagne solidaires n°205, mars 2006, pp. 16–17

Porcher J., 2007, Ne libérez pas les animaux ! Plaidoyer contre un conformisme « analphabête ». Revue du MAUSS n°29 – deuxième semestre 2007, pp. 352–362

Porcher J., Tribondeau C., 2008. Une vie de cochon. Editions La Découverte

Porcher J. 2008. Ouvrière en production porcine industrielle: le prix de la reconnaissance. Ethnographiques.org, n°15, février 2008. En ligne http://www.ethnographiques.org/2008/Porcher.html

Porcher J., 2009a. Bêtes de somme. Ravages n°3 « Adieu bel animal », Editions Descartes, pp. 115–135

Porcher J., 2009b. Le challenge de « cochons d'or », pilier défensif et maître étalon de la filière porcine industrielle. Economie rurale n°313–314, pp. 163–170

Porcher J., 2010. Cochons d'or. L'industrie porcine en questions. Editions Quae

Porcher J., Schmitt T., 2010. Les vaches collaborent-elles au travail ? Une question de sociologie. Revue du MAUSS n°35, premier semestre 2010. « La gratuité »

Porcher J., 2010. Le stade ultime des productions animales: la viande in-vitro. La Revue Politique et Parlementaire. Europe : quelle PAC pour 2013. n°1057. Oct–Nov 2010, pp. 97–104

Porcher J., 2011. Mettre au jour la place des animaux dans le travail. In Dans Béguin P., Dedieu B, Sabourin E., 2011. Le travail en agriculture. Son organization et ses valeurs face à l'innovation. L'Harmattan

Rault J.J., 2004. Une nuit avec les ramasseurs de volailles . Film. Production Jean-Jacques Rault. Icomtec, 2004

Reagan T., 1985. The case for animal rights. University of California Press

Roudart L., Mazoyer M., 1997. Histoire des agricultures du monde. Du néolithique à la crise contemporaine. Le Seuil

Sahlins M., 1980. Critique de la sociobiologie. Aspects anthropologiques. Gallimard

Saint Simon H., 1851. Du système industriel. Introduction Editions

Salmona M., 1994a. Les paysans français. Le travail, les métiers, la transmission des savoirs. Editions L'harmattan, 372 p

Salmona M., 1994b. Souffrances et résistances des paysans français. Editions L'Harmattan, 254 p

Sanson A., 1858. Les missionnaires du progrès agricole. Librairie de L. Hachette et Cie

Sanson A., 1907. Traité de zootechnie. Tome I. Librairie agricole de la Maison rustique. Cinquième édition

Senett R., 2000. Le travail sans qualités. Les conséquences humaines de la flexibilité. 10/18. Albin Michel

Serpell J., 1986. In the company of animals. Basil Blackwell. UK

Sigaut F., 1988. Critique de la notion de domestication. L'Homme n°108, pp. 59–71

Sinclair U., 2003/1906. La jungle. Editions Mémoire du livre

Singer P., 1993. La libération animale. Grasset

Singer P., 2004. Comment vivre avec les animaux. Les Empêcheurs de penser en rond

Sloderdijk P., 2003. Ni le soleil, ni la mort. Jeu de piste sous forme de dialogues avec Hans-Jürgen Henrichs. Editions Pauvert

Sloterdijk P., 2000. Règles pour le parc humain. Editions Mille et une nuit

Sorente I., 2011. Addiction générale. Lattès

Stengers I., 2003. 100 mots pour commencer à penser les sciences. Les Empêcheurs de penser en rond

Straus E., 2000/1935. Du sens des sens. Editions Jérôme Millon

Tapper R. L., 1994. Animality, humanity, morality, society, dans. In Tim Ingold (ed.), What is an animal ? Routledge. UK

Thomas K., 1985. Dans le jardin de la nature. La mutation des sensibilités en Angleterre à l'époque moderne (1500–1800). NRF. Gallimard

Thomas L.V., 2000. Les chairs de la mort. Corps, mort, Afrique. Préface de Jean-Marie Brohm. Les empêcheurs de penser en rond

Thomas L.V., 1980. Le cadavre. De la biologie à l'anthropologie. Editions Complexe

Thomson E.P., 1851. The passions of animals. Bradbury and Evans printers. London. Ouvrage numérisé par Google, disponible sur internet

Thomson E.P., 2004. Temps, discipline du travail et capitalisme industriel. La Fabrique Editions

Tort P. (dir.), 1985. Misère de la sociobiologie. PUF

Veyret P., 1951.Géographie de l'élevage. Gallimard

Vialles N., 1987. Le sang et la chair. Les abattoirs des pays de l'Adour. Editions Maison des Sciences de l'Homme

Vincent J.C., 1997. La mise à mort des animaux de boucherie: un révélateur des sensibilités à l'égard des bêtes à l'époque contemporaine. Cahiers d'Histoire, 42, 3–4

Vissac B., 2002. Les vaches de la République. Editions Quae
Vovelle M., 1973. Mourir autrefois. Gallimard
Waal de F., 1995. Collection Opus. Editions Odile Jacob
Waal de F., 2010. L'âge de l'empathie : leçons pour une nature enfin apaisée. Editions Les Liens qui Libèrent
Williams B., 1990. L'éthique et les limites de la philosophie. NRF. Gallimard
Zeuner F.E., 1963. A history of domesticated animals. Hutchinson, London

Index

Note: Page numbers with “n” denote footnotes.

J. Porcher, *The Ethics of Animal Labor*,
DOI 10.1007/978-3-319-49070-0